As I Recall:

Memories From A Lifetime In Dade County

Rex A. Blevins

ISBN: 1537127217
ISBN-13: 978-1537127217

DEDICATION

To my parents: Allison and Maggie Blevins

CONTENTS

Acknowledgments   i

Editor's Introduction   iii

1   Rex Blevins' Childhood Stories   1

2   The Jail Years: 1955-1972   13

3   Blevins Family Stories   47

4   People of New England, GA   59

5   Blevins Ancestry: 1800-1991   92

6   Appendix: Photos   110

ACKNOWLEDGMENTS

I want to thank Joshua Hall, Chris Musser, and Kent Woodrow for their help and encouragement in my life, and their support of this project. Thank you to Amy Hall for supplying the title for this work.

EDITOR'S INTRODUCTION

I have been honored to know Rex Blevins for more than ten years. His stories have had me laughing more times than I can count. Dade County has been home to his family for more than a century.

The stories which follow are important because they give us a glimpse into Dade County's past. In reading them we are transported into a time not long ago, not unlike our own, a time filled with hard work, practical jokes, tragedies, and dear friends and family. Unlike some books, these accounts are about real people, they really happened, at least this is the way Rex Blevins remembers them happening. These are the great American tales; stories which will make you laugh, stories which will make you cry. Most importantly, these are stories which will make you love Dade County a little bit more.

Also throughout this book are photos and facts which tell the story of Dade County at least as vividly as do the stories about Rex and his friends and family.

In editing this work I have tried not to take away from the charm with which Rex uses words. I have merely edited for clarity and helped with arranging, formatting and publishing issues.

It is my hope that you will find this work as charming as I did.

Joshua M. Hall

REX BLEVINS' CHILDHOOD STORIES

HAPPY DAYS AT SCHOOL

The following short stories happened in school during sixth through twelfth grades. Some are believable and some you may not believe. I can assure you all these things really happened. Few, if any, of the teachers are with us anymore. They were all good teachers and cared enough about us that they put up with all our meanness and continued to pound knowledge into our heads.

We moved into the new Dade County High School in 1956. Today it is the elementary school right behind the jail. There was a big to-do about the school being built so close to the jail. Some people were concerned about the students walking by the jail, about what the kids might hear coming from the prisoners. I reminded people that I lived in the jail and I assured them that the prisoners heard worse things from the student mouths.

Now back to my stories. Jimmy was new at our school. The new building had no identification names on the doors. I should point out that Jimmy was sort of bashful and his face turned red at the drop of a hat. Everyone knew which bathroom was the girl's and which the boy's, except Jimmy. He asked us where the boy's bathroom was. Naturally we pointed straight across the hall to the girl's. The crowd gathered to watch the exit after he went in. Twelve girls came screaming out, and then Jimmy came out. You could have lit a cigarette on his face it was so red! To show our gratitude for the laugh, we gave him a round of applause. Jimmy was such a good sport he finally joined in the laughter after the shock wore off.

The school was full of crazy people. It was the type that everyone still loved. This story just proves my point. The weather was freezing and someone suggested we open all the windows before the teacher came in. There were 10 or 12 windows, top and bottom in the room. The teacher walked in and the class sat there as if it was 90 degrees outside and it was ok to open the windows. The teacher begged the class to close or help close the windows. No one moved. Half way through the closing Mr. C. got one of those dreaded collapsing medal chairs we set up in every room. When someone sat or stood in one, it would just fall apart. When it fell Mr. C grabbed for the top window and with his feet dangling in midair yelled for help. Did anyone get up to help him up or close the windows? Well no, we just sat there and pretended we did not know anything. Did I not say we were crazy!! When we were asked who did it no one knew anything.

Before the Supreme Court ruled you could not read the Bible and pray, we always started school with Bible reading and prayer. We always took turns. Bobby was one of the smarter classmates in our class. On Bobby's day he got through the reading and was supposed to lead us in the Lord's Prayer. You know how it begins with "our Father which"? Bobby's did not start out this way. He began "the Lord is my shepherd". Before he could finish, the room cleared. Bobby and the teacher were the only ones left in the room. He died right there in front of the class. It took weeks before we let him forget it. We were a cruel class and never passed up a chance to torment someone. He said "I just could not remember the Lord's Prayer."

2

Russell pulled the wildest chair collapsing stunt. He sat a chair up at the teacher's desk. The teacher called the roll and proceeded to put the roll in the desk. All of a sudden the chair collapsed and the teacher disappeared under the desk with only his feet sticking out from under the desk. Everyone just sat there thinking how normal the situation was. We wanted to laugh, but we dared not laugh out loud, since we could have been sent to the office.

I will not take credit for this, but it was funny at the time. Someone brought some small cherry bombs that you set off by stomping on them or throwing them against the floor. Someone thought it would be a great idea if four of them were taped to the bottom the teacher's chair legs. Our teacher always used to flop down and sit on one leg. When he hit the chair the bombs went off and he flat footed on one leg to the top of the desk. We didn't even get a chance to laugh because he sat right down and started teaching the class as if nothing had happened. This teacher was one of the smartest teachers we had and still we abused his authority. This was the first and last time this trick was pulled, but it was still funny. He knew not to ask who did it because he knew he would not get an answer.

I know we should not have tortured our teachers, but what can I say? That was 50 years ago. Well back to the stories.

Someone had brought some rubber vomit to school. I went into Mr. C.'s class and placed it on the center of his desk. He would not sit at his desk. He spread newspaper over the rubber object on his desk. After class I got several people to gather around him until I could get the vomit out the door. He removed all the newspaper and looked everywhere for the blob of rubber vomit, but never found it.

TEACHER KICKS CAN

In sixth grade our teacher was an alcoholic. It took most of the school year for everyone except our class to realize he came to school drunk just about every day.

He had a bad leg he said he received in the army. He used to kick a gallon can he kept in our room when he got mad at us or wanted to get our attention. One day he was really upset and drunk. I think while he was passed out at his desk we were ripping the room apart and woke him up. He jumped up yelling he was faking sleep to catch us acting up. He ran over to his can drew back his bad leg and proceeded to kick it. There was one small difference this time. Someone had put a brick in the can and covered it with paper.

He bolted out the door and that the last we saw of him that day. The next day he went down each row and asked who put that brick in the can. You guessed it; no one knew or would tell him who did it. To this day I still do not know who put the brick in the can.

Later on that year he got drunk and hugged a pot belly stove in his home and it caused third degree burns over most of his body. We never saw or heard from him again. We did not learn anything that year, but we did have a good time in his class.

REVEREND KEN

Ken had a habit of acting out an Oral Roberts routine. Oral was a healing preacher. Ken would catch people at the water fountain and grab them by the top of the head and yell "heallllllll!" This went on in the hall way, lunch room and on the bleachers at the football field. I have no idea how many times he healed Mary Jane. Most people would see him coming and turn and run from him. This did not always work. Most were afraid lighting was going to strike them dead any minute.

TEACHER "TURKEY"

We nicknamed one of our teachers 'Turkey'. We often gobbled in the hallways by his room. One day 'Turkey' sneaked around and rushed into the hallway. Ken and a few others were in the hallway. 'Turkey' grabbed Ken and dragged him down the hall toward the office. Begging all the way, Ken tried to explain that it was not him who gobbled. The teacher told Ken if he would tell him who it was he would let him go. Ken told him it was his sister and another girl who shall remain nameless. These two were the meekest, shyest and quietest girls in the school. Gobbling was not in their vocabulary, but you could not expect Mr. C. to know this. He grabbed the two and began to lip lash them unmercifully. The two girls broke down sobbing and screaming "it was not us." Ken laughingly let the poor souls take the blame. I doubt Mr. C. ever knew the difference.

On another occasion, someone baked sweet potatoes in the lunch room. There were two long potatoes that looked a lot like, well, you know, like crap. The next time we all saw them was on Mr. C.'s desk crossed in a salute for everyone to see. Out came the newspaper. When class was over Mr. C suggested someone did that on purpose. Up came the crowd and away went the potatoes. Again Mr. C. looked and looked for the taters, but found nothing.

ANOTHER PRANK

I got blamed and took the blame for a lot of things. Russ put teachers through a lot. This happened to a teacher who stayed with us only one year, and then left for Tennessee and taught for 30 years.

This new teacher showed up right out of college to teach at Dade County High School. We thought she was in the wrong field. We used to gather around her desk and make her very nervous. She used to cry at the drop of a hat. One day Russ stood up in class and said, "What is that on the flag pole?" After a close look teacher realized it was her pocket book and starting begging for someone to get her bag and bring it back. I thought it was nice of Russ to go get it since he was the one who ran it up the flag pole. You guessed it, most of us ran out of the room until it was over with. We were afraid the principle might show up.

DR. BOBBY RAULSTON

Bobby was in Trenton for our 30th class reunion. He was a well know doctor in Oklahoma City, OK. He was present at the hospital when the building was bombed and a lot of people died. He spent days helping people and patching them after that nut case bombed the building.

This story appeared in the Dade County Sentinel dated July 4, 1990.

Dr. and Mrs. Robert "Bobby" Raulston of Oklahoma City, OK, formerly of New England, learned a lesson in small town police work. Bobby was here for his 30th class reunion on June 30th. Our class graduated in 1960. He was visiting his old home place at New England and parked his car while looking for the spring where his family used to get their water. He wanted to take a jug back to Oklahoma for his kids.

The law "locked" him up instead. A concerned citizen or a nosey neighbor called the law after seeing a big car in the hollow. After a search, paying a tow charge and a good laugh, the couple returned to Oklahoma City. "Gosh, it was good to be back in Dade County, but don't go up in Hick's Hollow in a Cadillac without someone who lives in the area!" Bobby said.

Bobby thought this was a set-up by his classmates whom he believed did not like him anyway. It was sort of strange because the deputy that showed up was the husband of one of his classmates. But to my knowledge it was not a set-up. We went out to dinner with him and had a great time and several laughs.

This is just how our class was: always something good and bad happening all the time.

BULLY MEETS BRICK

What story is good without at least one bully? In the seventh grade I was bullied by a senior. The guy was sixth foot tall and weighed over 250 pounds. I had tried everything to get it stopped and no one would help. I decided to take matters in my own hands. We had classes in old army barracks that were given to the school from Ft. Oglethorpe. The library was in one of those buildings. Jimmy started in on me and I picked up a brick and proceeded to follow him into the library. When he went in my brick followed him in the door. The brick landed at the desk of the librarian and she jumped up and wanted to know who threw that brick. I went in and told her it was me and I was throwing it at Jimmy and I was tired of him picking on me. You know she did not say anymore and that was the last time Jimmy targeted me.

TEACHER SNIDER

One of the best things that happened to Dade County High School happened when Snider showed up to start our first chemistry department. She changed our school for the better. She was one of us.

She helped us make stink bombs, operated on cats, coached girls' basketball, and established a new teacher-student relationship that we never had before. She was always there for us. (P.S. the cat lived and had several litter of kittens.) She had a great influence on students and other teachers.

We did get on her nerves at times. We started a game called "hit it". When someone yelled "hit it" everyone would just hit the floor. The girls basketball team was not exempt from "hit it" especially at their practice. Snider did not like it, but she was a good sport about it. The only time we got in trouble was when someone yelled "hit it" in the halls during class change. It was really confusing when the hall was filled with student sitting down. That game did not last long, but it was fun while it did.

Snider was a great friend to a lot of students, including me and still is there for us anytime. Even when she married a Moore she was still Snider to us.

STUDENTS STRIKE OVER COACH

Headline in Chattanooga News Free Press April 26, 1958:

Dade Students Strike Over Coach; School Officials May Ask Warrants

We were way ahead of the times. This was long before protests were common. Most of the students walked out because they fired our coach. All we asked was why they fired him. Student did not question authority back them, but we did.

The following is a picture of the students on strike:

Striker with 'leader' Frankie Woodfin, a senior at Dade County High School, is shown on the shoulders of some of his followers in a strike in protest against the failure of the school board to renew the contract of Coach Delmas Freeman. There are 333 pupils in the high school. It was estimated that about 100 were on strike. The school closed for three days. Moore agreed to meet with the strikers and tell why the coach was fired. Needless to say a meeting was held with no answer as to why coach Freeman was let go. I was in the middle of this group. I am the one with the "d" on my coat. It was reported to the sheriff that "your son is involved in the strike." Luckily Dad agreed with the strike, so I did not get in trouble. Things finally settled down and school continued without anyone getting kicked out.

COACH AS TEACHER

One of our classes was taught by the football coach. Sometimes he was in the classroom but most of the time he was not. We usually did whatever we wanted. One day we decided to get one of the guys we disliked down on the floor and some girl's make-up on him. The coach showed up and we had Bobby down in the floor with Shirley's make up kit applying the "stuff". When the coach asked what was going on three of us boys were caught red handed and Shirley had to admit the make-up was hers. The boys got their butts whipped and Shirley got expelled for three days. Shirley refused to go home because she said her parents would kill her. The situation got worked out without her having to leave school. Bobby was sent to the bathroom to wash his face and the three of us went to the storage room for our beating.

TEACHER DATES SENIOR

We had a great group of teachers. Some were right out of college. They fit right in with the students. One of these teachers was even dating a senior. At that time teachers dating students was taboo. Those of us who found out had to take advantage of this situation. We told him we would tell the school board if he did not go along with our requests. We borrowed his car and used his gas, we dated together, and we made him get us into clubs where we were too young to go. One of these trips got me in trouble. We had a little too much to drink and I had to go back to our house, or should I say the jail were we lived. You may have already guessed: my mother met me at the door and smelled my breath. Living in the jail meant that my mother had a lot of experience smelling the breath of drunks. She sent me to my room, but she did not tell my dad the sheriff.

This did not stop us from blackmailing our teacher. (P.S. that couple got married and had two children. They are still together and both are retired teachers. I consider them very good friends.) He was a special teacher who did a great job teaching at Dade County High School.

HARVESTING SUGAR

There was, and still is, a large spring on our farm. It was part of a park that was plotted out in the original city layout of New England city. It was called Taylor Park. The spring was lined with large rocks cut out the hill around the park. The same rocks can be seen as the foundation of the brick church in New England.

Each fall we would harvest the sugar cane to make sorghum or molasses syrup. This was an all day and night project. The kids in the family, including me, roamed the field between the house and the spring. We had a mule turn the press to squeeze the juice out of the cane. It ran down a pipe into the pan where the juice was cooked and turned into molasses. The pan was about five feet wide with sections off so the juice would run up and down the pan. The juice was cooked after about six passes down the pan. When the juice was about half way down the pan someone would dip some out and put it on a 5 gallon can lid for us to eat. It would be about half syrup by then. It still had a great taste and made us look forward to the end result. Molasses was great on homemade biscuits with real cows butter. It is hard to explain the operation, but it was a great time in my life. This process is still being done on Sand Mountain and some Amish settlement in Delano, Tennessee.

OLD PERSPECTIVES ON INTEGRATION

My letter reproduced for you below appeared in the Dade County Sentinel on January 26, 1961. I wrote this letter while attending the University of Georgia. Racial conflict was at its height across the country.

Headline: Student At University Tells Integration Views

(Editor's Note: Rex Blevins, Son of Sheriff and Mrs. Allison Blevins, is one of several local young people attending the University of Georgia, scene of Georgia's first school integration. His remarks are most thought provoking.)

> To evaluate the segregation issue is a difficult assignment. You are in essence expecting me, a college freshman, to answer a problem so complex that the greatest minds in our country cannot reach a clear-cut decision.

> I am here watching while the oldest chartered state university in the country is integrated. Somehow I faced the situation with mixed emotions. The backbone of the old south is her tradition and now her oldest folkway is going by the boards. To preserve segregation and states right, our forefathers took up arms exactly one hundred years to the day that the University of Georgia was integrated.

> On the other hand, progress has made the United States of America the greatest nation on the face of the earth, and in these crucial times, more than any other time in our history, we badly need to progress, in giant steps.

The colored boy, Hamilton Holmes, is a very intelligent medical student, who someday could become one of our greatest physicians. Depriving him of his education would be cutting off our nose to spite your face.

If receiving his education was his main purpose, I might be able to accept him without qualms. But he is a martyr for his race, an employee of the NAACP, and viewing him in this light, I do not feel any sympathy for him.

In a school of 7,500 students, two Negro pupils are of very little significance. I have never seen either one of them and am not personally affected by their presence, but I view it as a slap against the principles and teachings of the south.

I am afraid the people in the north who authorized their admittance do not understand the colored situation we face in the south. Our state leaders took the only safe and sane course when they chose to obey rather than buck the federal legislation. They realized that a very large majority of the students would rather tolerate the presence of two Negroes than jeopardize their education.

Until Wednesday night's fracas, the demonstrations were jovial outlets of tensions. The march through town and other riots were conducted in the spirit of a panty raid or pep rally. Things have cooled down now and the worst is behind us. The students have accepted the situation with the maturity due their station in life and have settled into the groove of another quarter of academics.

There were no more problems in that quarter as far as I can remember. I do not recall even seeing those two students the rest of my freshman year. If anyone does not think race relations have changed, please read this letter again. I am amazed that I used to think this way!

THE JAIL YEARS: 1955-1972

TRAGIC DEATH OF THE SHERIFF

In 1955 we moved the farm to the Dade County Jail where we lived until 1972. We did not realize how much of a change it would make in our family. We did not know at the time, but that Dad's Great Papaw had been sheriff of Dade County from 1856 to 1873. One hundred and one years had passed since he took office.

Sheriff F.C. Graham died about 1 pm in a Chattanooga hospital as a result of serious injuries received in November 1955 from an automobile accident. He had been unconscious since the time of the accident.

Many were hopeful during the sheriffs last days. Several Dade Countians donated blood in an effort to help save his life, but he had extensive brain damage which eventually took his life. He was also suffering from a mangled arm.

Sheriff Graham had been the police chief at Valley Head and had served as a police officer in Fairyland, Georgia, Crossville, Alabama, and Trenton, Georgia before his election as Dade County sheriff in 1952. He also operated a service station here for two years. He was survived by his wife, Mrs. Cordelia Johnson Graham, three sons Douglas, Felix, John; daughters

Mrs. James Bauback and Mrs. John Lake, and brothers Wesley and Oscar.

It was announced by R.M. Morrions, the Ordinary, that upon agreement of Charles T. Sims, coroner, Sims would act as sheriff until a special election could be held. He agreed and was then assisted by Bill Norton and J.G. Gilley who were appointed special deputies.

Dad decided to run for sheriff. He came home to our house in New England, Georgia, to ask mother what she thought of the idea. I never figured out why he asked her because he had already decided to run. What an experience it turned out to be! There was a candidate from every section of the county running.

Late news flash! Withdrawals from sheriff's race:

Ray Blackstock, who announced his candidacy for sheriff was not qualified to run as a candidate due to his age. Roy l Weather, also withdrew from the race. It was found that C.P. Whitt is a resident of Walker County and Mrs. F.C. Graham is not a registered voter in Dade County. Therefore their names will not appear on the ballot. This leaves 13 still in the race. J.H. Baty, Allison Blevins, J.O. Broome, Ozell Clark, Harold Cox, G.V. Green, W.H. Hartman, J.W. Lynch, Dan Massengale, Ike Moore, Bill Norton, Rushel Smith and Marvin Williams.

Dad was lucky enough to win the special election. After the votes were tallied, and Dad was declared the winner, we all piled into the 1953 Chevy, and headed to see the jail. We walked in the front door of the place and Mother informed Dad that he could move up there by himself, but that she and the kids would be staying in our house in New England!

The upstairs, where the prisoners were housed, was in better shape than the living quarters downstairs! In one of the bedrooms one of the former sheriff's sons had written his name in crayon. This had been there for years. The word "paint" had not been spoken by anyone, as you could easily see. The floors were "early boards and dirt." What made things ten times worse was mother was a fanatic when it comes to cleaning!

After the initial shock of seeing the place, the Ordinary (probate judge) at that time told Dad that he would get someone to paint, and that they could pick out rugs for the floors. George Cureton did most of the work cleaning up the place. For all the negative aspects, however, the one major advantage they spotted right off was the bathroom. In 1955, the Blevins' had not yet experienced indoor plumbing. We thought we had died and gone to heaven! The bathtub in the jail was one that sat up on legs and was a lot deeper than the wash tubs in which we were used to taking baths. Eventually that tub was taken out of the jail. No one knows why or what happen to it after it was removed from the jail.

We were to move in January of 1956, even though Dad's official duties started after the special election. The night of his election Dad's first arrest, if you can believe it, was Mother's cousin. The cousin had sort of celebrated too much and gotten a little too drunk.

This was a very exciting time for the whole family. Dad had a lot to learn about how to run the sheriff's office, and the rest of the family would experience aggravation, disappointment, and excitement in the next seventeen years Dad was to remain in office.

SHERIFF BLEVIN'S FIRST CAR

Dad purchased a car in 1954 or 1955. This was our first car and the car he used as his first sheriff's car. It was the first car I can remember. Up to this point we used a farm truck for all our traveling and farm work.

OUR FIRST VACATION

We took our first vacation the year before Dad ran for sheriff. We went to Florida. It was our first trip of more than 100 miles away from New England.

We took most of our food (home grown meat, eggs and vegetables) with us. We used a small gas stove for cooking on the way down. Just before entering Florida, we stopped along the side of the road to cook breakfast. Mother cooked country ham. You could smell it a mile away! There wasn't much traffic on the road at that time of the morning. One car came zooming by us and went passed us several blocks. He stopped and turned around and come flying back. He whipped into where we were and asked if we were cooking country ham. Dad told him yes. He said he would give anything for one bite of that ham. Dad asked him if he would like to join us for breakfast. "I sure would" was his reply. Can you imagine doing something like that this day and time? He ate and we never saw him again.

Here are four pictures of the courthouse built in 1927:

Courthouse – Trenton, Ga.

Note: This fence now surrounds the old Baptist cemetery in Trenton.

TRENTON, GEORGIA

BLEVINS MOVE TO JAIL

When we moved into the jail we attempted to settle down to what would become a normal life for the Blevins family. We celebrated our first of 17 Christmases. We started our jobs of answering the telephone, and operating the radio dispatching the sheriff on regular calls. Mother's new job was doing the cooking for us and the prisoners. I have been asked a hundred times what we ate at the jail. My standard answer was "we all ate of the same pots."

Mother's sister Dorothy (Doe Doe) came every day to help with the cooking and clean up. She was a great help during the time she work there. She helped all 17 years we occupied the jail.

The first year went by fast. The special election was just the start. Dad had to run in a regular election to stay in office. With the help of the GBI, state patrol, and the FBI Dad and all of us learned how to run the jail and the office of sheriff.

We got used to Dad bringing drunks, mattresses being set on fire and broken commodes and water running down on our clothes in our closets. The yelling of the drunks and fighting upstairs was just part of our new life. We never actually got used to it, but we learned to live with it.

Before we moved I was attended Morganville School and was in the sixth grade. In January I was moved to Trenton Elementary where met another group that would end up being our class of 1960. What a great move that was.

CHATEAU CLUB RAIDED

Lookout Mountain 1959 - Headlines: Georgia Deals with the Chateau Club

This club was located on Scenic Highway and what is now part of Covenant College. It was one block south of the Lookout Mountain hotel that had been a part of Lookout Mountain View for years.

Georgia revenue authorities and Dade County Sheriff Allison Blevins and his men are to be commended for their raid Saturday night on the blight that has grown up on the Georgia end of Lookout Mountain in the form of a joint call the chateau.

The chateau has by no means been a cheap joint. It is rather elaborated, but a joint all the same. It brought to this community an unwholesome influence by providing wide open gambling in violating of the law.

The raiding officers said they confiscated six slot machines, a gambling device that looks like and is called a "bird cage" in which three dice are tumbled, several gambling tables, and 21 fifths of liquor. (Note of interest the bird cage was recently given to covenant college to display as part of their history.) While the raid was in progress, a Chattanoogan identified as Raymond Bennett reportedly drove into the club parking lot with 23 fifths of stamped liquor in his car. Resulting in confiscation of the automobile and a change against him of transporting and possessing liquor in a dry county, Sheriff Blevins said he planned to take out warrants against the reputed operator of the chateau, Ernest B (Buster) Stanger, charging him with possession of gaming devices and liquor.

Most Chattanoogans have no desire for this community to become a Las Vegas or a Phoenix City. Alert, effective law enforcement on every level is required to curb those who seek riches by imposing a parasitic evil on the community in violation of the law.

Stanger was indicted as a result of the raid on the chateau club, swank night spot on Lookout Mountain. Buster Stanger's day in court resulted in him receiving 18 months in Georgia work camp and fines. He is appealing his conviction.

Attorney Bobby Lee Cook told the court that the state had failed to prove that Stanger owned or operated the place. He also argued that there was no proof that Sheriff Allison Blevins of Dade County, who led the raid, actually had talked to Stanger when he called a number listed in Stanger's name.

The sheriff made two calls to obtain instructions on how to open a locked closet in which the liquor was found. Cook contended the trial court erred in admitting evidence about the phone calls. Cook also said the state did not show that the defendant held legal title to the premises of the chateau supper club or that he had any lease hold or other interest therein.

Blevins testified that he called the number listed in Stanger's name twice to obtain instruction on how to open the locked closet and on the second call a man told him where to find a screwdriver to open the door.

This being quite foreign to Buster Stanger's taste, he much preferring more plush surroundings, his lawyer has moved for a retrial.

SHERIFF BLEVINS FACES FUGITIVE

The following happened to our family in March of 1959. We had been in the jail for four years when dad (Sheriff Allison Blevins) was involved in the capture of William Smothers who had escaped from Kirby Prison in Montgomery, Alabama.

The day started off with the normal telephone calls, prisoners being fed by my mother, sitting around waiting for the next telephone call and waiting for prisoners to be bonded out of jail.

Then around 12 noon the call came in from a resident in Wildwood, Georgia that a man was on the railroad near Highway 299 and Highway 11 who fit the description of the escapee from Alabama. All law enforcement agencies in the tri-state area were alerted. All vehicles going into Chattanooga were stopped and searched. Blood hounds were used and a helicopter was sent out to search the area. After the call to Dade County Sheriff's office the search was called off.

Dad and Trenton Chief of Police H. H. Hutchins (Hot Rod) took off and spotted Smothers leaning against a group of mailboxes. The Sheriff's car was marked in large letters as the two approached Smothers. Dad drove up besides the escapee and stopped.

Smothers was on the Sheriff's side of the car and as Dad opened the door to get out, Smothers raised his arm and pointed a pistol at Dad. As he did, Hot Rod who was on the other side of Dad fired. His shot hit Smothers in the left shoulder going through his body to his right side. This account puts to rest the other stories

22

that are out there about Dad being inside the car. Dad and Hot Rod were not in the car. Hot Rod shot Smothers and the shot went right by Dad's head. I recall Dad saying he could not hear out of his right ear for a long time for this reason. Dad left Hot Rod with his prisoner and went to call an ambulance which arrived about the same time as the Tennessee police. Smothers died on the operating table that night.

The big talk in the county the week after all this went down, was of the capture by Dade County law enforcement officers of the escaped convict from Alabama. The story was not only carried for several days in the Chattanooga papers but by United Press in the papers throughout the country.

A life of crime that began when he was child was brought to a close when William Smothers was buried beside his mother in Henagar Alabama. Funeral services for this escapee were attended by a large crowd at the Baptist Church in Henagar.

He had kidnaped four persons, stolen a car and drove all into Northeast Alabama. The hostages, including a terrified couple, a state trooper and a prison trustee, were release after being held by Smothers for 14 hours.

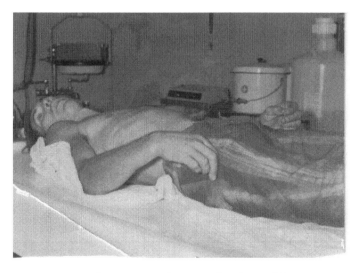

The fugitive on the examination table.

23

My family was sitting at the jail unaware of what was going on in Wildwood. We had heard that someone was shot, but we were not told who. We were thankful to hear it was Smothers and not Dad or Hot Rod. After this ordeal things settled down: DUIs, Speeders, Family Fights, Murders, and Moonshine Stills. The Moonshine was a big part of Dad's time in office. We did not think about the danger Dad faced every day he was in office from 1955 to 1972. He was surely blessed and protected by a higher power.

10TH GRADE BRIDE

The street that ran by the jail had great families that lived on it. One family was the Woodfins. We had lots of fun just hanging around. The jail yard was a great gathering place for a lot of teenagers.

One of the families lived on the next street. This girl was planning to get married. She was in the 10th grade. Rosemary and I took it upon our self to talk her out of it. Rosemary who lived right behind the jail came to my bed room window picked on the window and told me to come out. "Let's go and talk Karan out of getting married". I sneaked out of the jail leaving the front door unlocked. We spent several hours trying to talk her out of marriage to no avail. We both left to go home. When I got back to the jail mother had got up and locked the front door. I had to beat on the door to get back in. Mother opened the door and proceeded to chew me out and wanted to know where I had been. I told her and she had an "I don't believe you" look on her face. After that I went to bed and hoped Karan would change her mind. She did not and the rest is history.

REX DRAFTED

When I was drafted into the army in 1963, I left home (jail) to catch a Greyhound bus in front of Ann Other Flower Shop. Mother and Daddy were standing on the jail porch. I walked across the street with the instruction to my family not to cry when I got on the bus. I reminded them I was going to help protect our country. I had no idea there was a chance I could be sent to Vietnam. I went through basic training at Ft. Jackson, SC. I still did not think about Vietnam.

After basic and eight more weeks of special training I got my orders that I was going to the Whitehouse Communication Center. I was on cloud nine for about a week then my new order came through that I was going to the Pentagon.

I did not know what that entailed, but it did not sound too bad. In July 1964 I showed up in Washington, D.C. with my orders to report to the Pentagon. I spent the next two and a half years in the Joint Chief of Staff office processing message for the U.S. Army. It was a great ride. I met Jennifer, my wife to be and the mother of our three children: Craig, Leigh Ann and Amy who gave us six wonderful grandchildren.

TEENAGERS STOP ROBBERY

Headline: Quick Action on the Part of Two Dade County Teenagers Foiled a Robbery in the Pre-Dawn Hours

According to Dade County Sheriff Allison Blevins: Tommy Lawson and Jerry Henagar were passing by the Wildwood Post Office when they spotted three men trying to break into the building. The boys promptly called the sheriff's office giving a description of the car at the post office.

Sheriff Blevins and Buddy Crawford apprehended the three, jailing them until federal officers returned them to Tuscaloosa Jail where they had escaped. They were charged on three federal counts of car theft, carrying a sawed-off shotgun and attempting to rob a post office.

Sheriff Blevins commended young Lawson and Henagar for promptly reporting the incident.

BEA RUMLEY REWARDED BY FBI

Bea Rumley of the Georgia Game Park at Rising Fawn, was presented a $100 reward by special agent John J. Kiljan, U.S. Secret Service and Sheriff Blevins of Dade County.

Mrs. Rumley Given $100 Reward By FBI

A couple presented a twenty dollar counterfeit bill at the park. Mrs. Rumley was quick to detect the counterfeit bill and promptly called the sheriff's office. The couple was picked up and later carried to Rome, Georgia by the U.S. authorities.

A letter of commendation for her alertness accompanied the check from V.E. Baughman, Chief of the U.S. Secret Service, in which he expressed his appreciation for her outstanding assistance in the apprehension of the counterfeiters.

Appreciation was also expressed to Sheriff Blevins for his promptness in having the two apprehended.

FATHER KILLS SON

One of the saddest events during Sheriff Blevins' term was when a father beat his son to death with a crowbar. It happened at the Crisp home on Sand Mountain. The son had been severely beaten about the head and died in tri-county hospital. The crowbar was later found in the yard. The dad was arrested and charged with the death.

I have a memory of the sheriff having to go upstairs at the jail and telling the Dad what he had done to his son. I can still hear the father's screams when the sheriff told him.

What happened after this tragedy made this story even worse. The dad committed suicide because he was never able to deal with what he had done.

PAUL CRANE FOUND GUILTY

Jury finds Paul rate Guilty of Murder. Mercy was recommended, the sentence was life in hard labor.

Sheriff Allison Blevins was notified Monday by GBI agent Jim Hillman, who has been sought by authorities since his escape from Floyd County Jail, several months ago, in Salisbury North Carolina.

According to reports given by the sheriff, Crane told officers that he was "tired of running." He was accompanied by his daughter, Paulette, when he turned himself in.

Floyd County sheriff Joe Adams left for Salisbury to return Crane to Rome, Georgia. It is expected that the return trip will bring them through Trenton in order to leave the girl there.

SHERIFF AND CROWBAR—Dade County Sheriff Allisc Blevins is shown in his office at the county jail at Trento Ga., with a bloody crowbar found in the yard at the home (Troy Crisp, Trenton, Rt. 2. Crisp's son, Sherman H. Crisp, w: found in a bed in the house, severely beaten about the hea: Sherman Crisp died Wednesday morning, a few hours after h was discovered by Constable Floyd Patton.

Sheriff Blevins said that the time limit set for an appeal to be made in the life sentence Crane received here in 1956 had run out during the time Crane was at large.

The case went to jury at about 4 p.m. following lengthy interrogation of witnesses. Shortly before midnight, Judge Davis cleared the courtroom and had mattresses sent up for the jury. Col. and Mr. C.S. Williams invited solicitor Earl Self to spend the night at their Rising Fawn home rather than make the long trip back to Summerville. At about 1:15 a.m. Constable Russell

Young was sent to tell the judge the jury had reached a verdict. Their decision was read at 2 a.m.

The three-day trial, in which Crane was charged with murder in the brutal attack on Junius Nesbitt in October of 1951 from which the aged man died, attracted many spectators who kept the courtroom crowded except when the testimony by a succession of witnesses grew overlong and repetitious.

Crane was represented by attorneys Andrew Cain, D.L. Lomenick and Joe Wild, Jr. who used an alibi defense. Crane contended that he was elsewhere at the time the crime was committed. Solicitor Earl B. Self built up a strong case for the state, bringing to the stand over a dozen witnesses, including FBI agent, J. P. Hillan.

Part of Hillan's testimony recorded the fact that on his first visit to Mr. Nesbitt in a Chattanooga hospital, which was on the day following the attack victim's admittance to the hospital, Mr. Nesbitt was rational and stated that two of his attackers were Paul Crane and Milt Lee. The other two he did not recognize.

"I'll never make it". Mr. Nesbitt told the agent, "I'll never get out of this hospital." He died later from combined causes, including brain and liver damage, pneumonia and bruising, all from the attack. This cause of death was stated by Dr. Augustus Mccraverk who was called in by attending physicians to examine Mr. Nesbitt. Dr. Mccravey was a witness for the defense.

Part of the state's evidence was a series of testimonies which painted a scene of ruthless torture. Several witnesses described the blood spattered about, the burned newspapers near a rocking chair, and the ransacked house.

One of the state's outstanding witnesses was Jimmy Lee, Alias Carroll Franklin, who stated that Paul told him he got Mr. Nesbitt's money. Upon cross examination the defense attempted to prove that Lee, with his younger brother who was also a witness, was trying to "make things easier" for his father, Milt Lee. The elder Lee, now serving a life term for the crime, was brought to the Trenton jail for the trial, but was not called to the stand. Jimmy Lee was acquitted of the crime at the same trial during which his father was convicted.

A key witness for the defense was Clyde Crane, brother of Paul. Around eight other witnesses were also called, some of them for the purpose of establishing the fact that Paul Crane was not well-known in Dade County. In his summary of the case before the jury, attorneys suggested that Mr. Nesbitt could not have known Paul Crane and therefore could not have recognized him by name.

The jurors who sat on the Crane case are as follows: J.B. Geddie, Jr., J. C. Wallen, R. H. Dabbs, Grady Wisenant, John T. Shelton, J. S. Parsons, William P. Burr, Claud E. Smith, Estell Robinson, Roy Higdon, l. L. Bridgeman and Bennie Ira Cole.

Paul Crane was sentenced to prison for life.

SHORT STORIES OF OUR TIME AT THE JAIL

When we moved to the jail, Linda and I were in our teen years. We were never sure what we could and could not do. Most of the time we just did what we wanted and faced the music later.

It was snowing in Trenton and I decided we should go outside on the jail steps and take a few pictures. So I told Linda to go put her bathing suit on and we would head out. While we were on the steps posing for pictures, cars were going by the jail and looking at two crazy people outside in the snow, Linda in her bathing suit. Traffic did not stop, but people stared.

After a few pictures, the sheriff came around the courthouse without our noticing him. He stopped beside the jail and informed both of us to get our butts back in the jail. Needless to say we put that behind us and did not try that stunt again. We thought it was funny, but Dad did not.

Speaking of Linda and the jail, the Busy Bee was a popular restaurant the square nearby. Linda and her friend Peggy Gifford decided to go down and entertain the customers at the Busy Bee. They donned a pair of Daddy's overalls and hats and marched into the restaurant and proceeded to sing the song "Waterloo, Waterloo." Peggy sang through her nose which made the song even better. Try to sing it and see for yourself. I think there were pictures made, but I have no idea where they are. Luckily Daddy did not see them until it was over. I am surprised daddy got elected four times!

We never knew for sure how many were in jail each day. Dad would bring in people day and night. Mother would go to the small trap door in the metal door and open it and yell, "how many are up there," then she and Doe Doe would know how many to fix breakfast for.

My friend would come to the jail when we wanted to see each other. One of the events we did often was play badminton. The prisoners were our cheering section. How many people can say that?

My mother loved to watch the Friday night fights. Her cousin was in jail by himself, so she would let him out and he would watch the fight with her. After they were over at 10, she would lock him back up. Talk about your Mayberry R.F.D. - we had it in Dade County!

I was at the jail one day when someone ran up to the jail and told me there was smoke coming out of the windows. I opened the trap door and asked the prisoners what was going on. They had set some mattress on fire in the bull pin, a big cell with 8 bunk beds. "What's going on up there?" I shouted. "Rex come up here and get us out of here." they replied. I crawled up the steps and over to the bull pen and carefully opened the doors. They ran out like a herd of sheep jumping over me while I was lying on the floor. I was so upset that I told them they could just smother to death next time. We got the fire out and threw the mattress outside with the help of some men on the street.

One of my classmates in high school was in jail, so I pulled up a chair by the door and had a conversation with him. I tried to find out what happened and why he went the way he was. We were raised in New England and he seemed to have no problems as a kid. But he was eventually killed in Louisiana.

The sheriff brought in a drunk and was taking him upstairs. He could not walk so Dad was pushing him up the steps. The prisoner was about half up the steps when he kicked Dad in the mouth like a mule. Dad took his flap jack out (piece of metal covered with leather) and proceeded to beat the guy's ass. The next morning Dad went upstairs to take the man over to the judge's office to get a bond set. He told the sheriff "I don't know what I was drinking yesterday, but the cheeks of my ass are so sore I can't sit down. He didn't seem to notice that Dad's lip was busted!

LIGHT HEARTED STORIES OF THE JAIL

Jay showed up at the jail to ask Mother for Linda's hand in marriage. We were all sitting in the living room of the jail. We sat and sat until late in the night. I knew what was going on, but Mother had no idea.

After a while I got up and went into the kitchen and yelled for Mother. "Mother would you come in here a minute". Mother came into the kitchen and I told mother "go back into the living room and bring up the subject of marriage." Jay wants to ask for Linda's hand. Mother said are you sure? "Yes I am. It is late and I have to go to school in the morning."

So mother went back into the living room and brought up the subject. I can still see the relief on Jay's face. So after that Jay asked, Mother approved, he left, we all went to bed and the rest is history.

I was always hard to wake up in the morning in time for school. This was the case from first grade. Mother would start yelling at me to get up and get ready to go to school. She did her yelling every morning from the kitchen while she was fixing breakfast for the prisoners.

She usually ended up in my room with a fly swat to get my attention or wake me up. Sometimes I would just lay there and not move, this would drive her up the wall. She usually won the fight and I would get up and get ready for school. I usually had to run the half block to make it to class on time.

One morning I decided to try and break mother from using the fly swat on me. I got up when she called me and fixed my pillows as if I was still in the bed. I hid behind the door and waited for her to come into my room. She came in slinging the fly swat and proceeded to beat the pillows.

After several swats I jumped out from behind the door and grabbed her by the ribs. She yelled, I yelled and she thought one of the prisoners had grabbed her. Luckily I was completely dressed so I did not run out into the street without my clothes on. I ran out the door with her right behind me swatting me every step I took. I made it to school that day without being late. Needless to say that was the last time I tried that! I loved mother, but I always gave her a rough time.

1963 FREEDOM MARCHERS

A group of "freedom marchers" set out on the second leg of a walk through the Deep South as a protest against segregation. The march drew jeers and insults their first day out.

These freedom walkers in Dade County on way to Alabama
line were arrested and put in jail in 1959.

They are retracing the steps of Baltimore Postman William
Moore, who was shot to death near Attalla, Alabama.

Eight Negroes who planned a similar demonstration from Attalla
were arrested and charged with breach of the peace. They are
being held in jail at Gadsden, Alabama.

The freedom marchers who started their walk from Chattanooga,
Tennessee, spent the night huddled in sleeping bags and blankets

34

on the floor and pews of a little white frame church at Hooker, a northwest Georgia community.

The Mount Calvary Baptist Church is in the midst of a Negro community. But white persons live nearby, and some of them dropped into speak to the five white men and five Negro men. Most of them said they came because they were curious.

Dade County Sheriff Allison Blevins stopped briefly but declined to talk with newsmen. He had previously said that he was making no special arrangements for the marchers. I traveled to Hooker with Dad to see what was going on. Dad did offer the marchers a bus to take them through Dade County to the Alabama line. They refused his request. He told them it would be for their own protection.

The marchers met with jeers along the route from Chattanooga to the Tennessee line, about nine miles. Two Tennessee troopers in a patrol car accompanied them to the Georgia line. There were no officers on the Georgia side of the line. Most of the hecklers cried "nigger lover" at the marchers. A handful of rocks were thrown at the marchers from a car. Many Negroes along the highway waved gaily. Five of the marchers are members of the congress of racial equality and five belong to the student non-violent coordinating committee.

When the marchers arrived at the Alabama line they were beaten and arrested by the Alabama state troopers.

ROBBERY AT THE RED FOOD STORE

Hearkening back to the days of the "old west" three armed robbers held up the Red Food Store and fled with an undetermined amount of money following a reported exchange of gunfire.

Headed by sheriff Allison Blevins, who was immediately called to the scene, a tristate alert was issued. As reported by eye-witnesses, three white men wearing ski masks staged the armed robbery in which they systematically looted the cash registers and safe before fleeing in a blue Ford automobile.

Sheriff Blevins reported later that the car was found abandoned in the Murphy's Hollow area, some seven miles north of Trenton. The vehicle identified as the getaway car was reported stolen from the parking lot of Tri-County Hospital, Fort Oglethorpe, on the day before the holdup.

Law enforcement officers in Georgia, Alabama and Tennessee were alerted in the search for the armed robbers who were believed to have continued their flight. Sheriff Blevins said they could find no clues. It was obvious that the thieves were very familiar with the store and had planned the holdup carefully.

One of the customers in the store during the robbery was Jack Blevins. Jack was well known for his ability to tell tales and add something to make them funny.

He told the sheriff that after the robbery happened he was so afraid that he ran out of the store and proceeded down Highway 11. He stated that when he got to Atkin's store (which was across from present Four Fields) he threw up his hand to turn off the highway and only then realized that he was not even in his truck!

MOONSHINE

Headline: 750-Gallon-a-day still in Dade County Raided By Agents, 2 Men Arrested.

Georgia and federal agents raided a large still in the Wildwood community. The still had three metal pots containing some 2400 gallons of mash and was capable of running off some 750 gallons of moonshine per day. Two men were found at the still and were taken into custody following a short but speedy chase though the wooded section.

By using a portable tank of butane gas, the mash was heated and its vapors carried by pipe through a condenser make of two automobile radiators where it was turned into the liquid form of alcohol. Dead rats, snakes, bugs and leaves were found in the mash. There was a thick film of slime over the two radiators.

A preliminary test on the finished product indicated the uncut whiskey was about 150 proof alcohol and took about eight hours to make. Before leaving the area, the agents used knives and axes to puncture the jugs and knock holes in several metal drums found at the scene. They also ignited some sticks of dynamite charges that left the large stills in ruins.

Agent Williams looked at a sample of the moonshine which was filled with debris and said," I can't see how anyone could drink this stuff if they knew how it was made."

In the 1950's and 1960's and prior, Dade County was known for their "moonshine". It was sold locally and in the Chattanooga area. Now "shine" is making a comeback. It is being made to taste better by putting apples and other fruit in it. It is also being sold in whiskey stores all over the country.

The biggest thing that changed moonshine making was when the bootleggers changed from wood burning to propane gas. The revenuers could not see the smoke to locate the stills. After this they had to follow the smell. The sheriff got the nickname of "sniffer" because he could be driving down the road and sniff out a still. It worked too!

This report will include just a few of the stills the sheriff and revenue agent found in Dade County and destroyed. Several times I went with them to the woods to destroy stills and help carry out evidence.

NOVEMBER 1961 TWO SURPRISE RAIDS NET LIQUOR, DRUG CATCHES.

Georgia State A.T.U. agents Jim Mashburn and Jess Scoggins found a nest of five 15,000 gallon capacity, ground hog-type stills lined up in a row beside a peaceful mountain stream about a mile off the Cloudland Highway. Ground hog stills are stills partially buried in the ground. After notifying Sheriff Allison Blevins, the agents explored further and discovered another nest of five. The stills were set up to be run each day with a capacity of 1000-gallons per week.

The agents along with Sheriff Blevins, Joe Blevins and Bill Breedlove destroyed the stills and confiscated 225 gallons of "white lightin'", and destroyed 11,500 gallons of mash found at the stills according to Sheriff Blevins.

A raid staged by Sheriff Allison Blevins on midway café apparently confirmed suspicions that drugs were being sold in Dade County. A large quantity of drugs was found on the premises. This truck stop, located about six miles south of Trenton, was owned by John Murray, a former Florida resident. Murray was arrested and pled guilty to charges of illegal sale of whiskey, possessing beer for resale and possessing whisky.

WHISKEY STILLS RAIDED – 1959

A prize of war on moonshine is exhibited by sheriff Allison Blevins and deputy Bill Breedlove. A moonshine still in operation and eight barrels of mash were seized on Sand Mountain on December 19, 1959, by Georgia alcohol tax men and Dade County deputies. Two men at the still escaped when the lawmen approached.

The still was in the vicinity of Wolf's Pen Gulf. Those making the raid were Deputies Bill Breedlove and Joe Blevins, and Jess Scoggins, State Officer.

The previous day Sheriff Allison Blevins and state officer W.H. Southers seized 30 gallons of non-tax paid whiskey in another section of Sand Mountain.

130 GALLONS SEIZED

A car containing 130 gallons of moonshine whiskey was seized by Constable Charles Green just off the "short cut" road on Sand Mountain. A well-known bootlegger was arrested with possessing non-tax-paid whiskey.

PRIZE OF WAR is exhibited by sheriff Allison Blevins and deputy Bill Breedlove. The still was captured in a raid on Sand Mountain. (Nickajack photo)

Whiskey Stills Raided

A moonshine still in operation and eight barrels of mash were seized on Sand Mountain Dec. 19 by Georgia alcohol tax men and Dade county deputies. Two men at the still escaped when the lawmen approached.

The still was in the vicinity of Wolf's Pen Gulf. Those making the raid were deputies Bill Breedlove and Jess Blevins and Jess Scoggins, state officer.

The previous day sheriff Allison Blevins and state officer W.H. Southers seized gallons of non-tax paid whiskey in another section of Sand Mountain.

130 Gallons Seized

A car containing 130 gallons of moonshine whiskey was seized by constable Charles green Saturday just off the "short cut" road on Sand Mountain. Doyle Stephens was jailed at Trenton under a $500 bond charged with possessing non-tax paid whiskey.

Capture Two Stills

Sheriff Allison Blevins and deputies cut down two stills on Sand Mountain Christmas Eve and found two 500 gallon pots, one ready to run and the other just loaded.

DADE SHERIFF RAIDS STILL

Dade County Sheriff Allison Blevins, along with federal and state alcoholic agents, raided a still recently on Sand Mountain. The

39

still consisted of two 1,000 gallon Alabama black pots. One of the units was running when officers made the raid. Raiding officers found and destroyed 52 gallons of whiskey. See the photo on the next page:

"WILDCAT" IS NO MORE JANUARY 25, 1962

Sheriff Allison Blevins poured out whiskey confiscated in a raid on a Sand Mountain home as Bill Breedlove stood by.

Fifty gallons of Wildcat Whiskey was confiscated and a still destroyed in a raid by Sheriff Allison Blevins and Constable Bill Breedlove. According to Sheriff Blevins the whiskey was seized at the home of a well-known bootlegger.

No one was home at the residence at the time of the raid. A warrant was issued for the owners of the home. The whiskey was poured into the Lookout Creek making the fish very happy and easy to catch.

41

CRIMP HURTS BUSINESS, BUT NOT THE JUGS.

Georgia put a crimp in one case of Tennessee's export 'business' here in Dade County.

The "crimping", however didn't bother the containers being used. Dade county officers confiscated a 1948 automobile carrying 61 jugs of moonshine whiskey – and all but one of the jugs were made of plastic.

TRENTON, GEORGIA   THURSDAY, JANUARY 25, 1962

ildcat" Is No More

riff Allison Blevins pours out whiskey confiscated in a raid on a Sand Mountain home as Bill dlove stands by.

(Times Staff Photo)

Sheriff Allison Blevins said "you could bounce them off a wall and not bother them a bit"

The officers arrested William Ellis Doyle, of Soddy, Tennessee, just after he left a restaurant on the square here. The Tennessee man told them he was carrying the whiskey to Alabama.

Sheriff Blevins said he became suspicious when he saw Doyle's car pass through Trenton earlier in the evening. He pursued him south on U.S. Highway 11, but lost him. Not finding him between Trenton and the Alabama line, Blevins returned here.

Just after his return, he spotted the car he had been following parked on the square. The sheriff and Constable Hutchison waited until Doyle left the restaurant (Busy Bee), then returned to the car and arrested him. In court he pled guilty and paid fines on traffic charges. He was bound over to the grand jury on the charge of transporting unstamped whisky.

SHERIFF ALLISON BLEVINS RECEIVES NATIONAL PEACE OFFICER RECOGNITION - 1961

We are featuring this week, Sheriff Allison Blevins; one of the most popular sheriffs ever elected in Dade County. He was elected to office six years ago and is described as a "hard man to beat" in an election. His honesty and devotion to duty has not gone unnoticed. He has earned the respect of not only the people of Dade County but state officers who work with him daily as well. In order to have an efficient law enforcement network, the state and county officials must work together as a team in such cases as the recent manhunt of three escapees and the December air crash, where sheriff Blevins and a state trooper guarded the plane until officials arrived to investigate the crash. This crash occurred on the Sells farm in Trenton.

Dade County is fortunate to have a sheriff like Allison Blevins who along with the help of his wife, Maggie Blevins perform the duties of the office with dignity and perseverance.

BOY SCOUTS RESCUED IN CAVE

This article was printed in the Washington Post in Washington, DC while I was stationed there in the army. It appeared on April 17, 1966.

Headline: 3 Scouts Saved in Cave; Leader, 2 Rescuers die.

Rescuers early pulled three Boy Scouts from a cave, but their leader who had been trapped with them for 12 hours was found dead, bringing to three the number to suffocate in the unexplored gas-filled Howard's cave near Trenton.

Officers led Chris Shannon 14, Mike Strickland, 15, and Doug Fleming, 16, all members of an Atlanta scout troop. A local victim that did not make it out was Benny Gilley.

The body of Bill Howell, 25, leader of the scouts, was found on the 50-foot ledge where the four had been trapped since an explosion earlier. Six other scouts escaped some time earlier.

Rescuers made contact with the trapped scouts six hours after the blast, as darkness was gathering in the mountains. They could hear the scouts, but not see them.

They were crouched on a ledge 20 feet about the cave floor, and 300 feet from its mouth. Poisonous gas, heavier than air, swirled beneath them.

It took four hours to bring in breathing apparatus big enough to take rescuers all the way to the scouts and back again. "we're coming in a minute," rescuers yelled to them, "just stay where you are and don't panic."

Rescuers near the mouth of the cave shouted their names-all okay! Seconds later the three stumbled out of the flood lite cave mouth, gulping hungrily at the cool night air.

All were wrapped in blankets, placed on stretchers and rushed to Chattanooga hospital. The cavern is filled with carbon dioxide gas, an officer said.

SHERIFF BLEVINS ARRESTED

Headline: Retired Sheriff Blevins, 83 1st 'Arrest' At New Dade County Jail, by Myrna McMahan.

In 17 years as Dade County's sheriff, Allison Blevins made many arrests. On Friday, he learned what it's like to be "on the inside, looking out."

The highly-respected, 83-year old former official was taken into custody by order of current Sheriff Philip Street, handcuffed and booked into Dade County's new $2 million jail and courthouse complex.

Actual charges were not clear at the time, but Sheriff Blevins seemed to enjoy the notoriety of being the first "prisoner" to be jailed in the new 48-bed facility, which is plush compared to the dilapidated old jail condemned by court officials in 1985.

Lt. Don Smith was assisted in the "collar" by Sgt. J. D. Debord, commander of the Lafayette state patrol post, and trooper J.D. Spurgeon, all of whom lightheartedly said the defendant gave them "some trouble."

He gave us some backtalk, and when we got him in the car he wouldn't get out-we had to pull him out in order to book him, Lt. Smith said.

"Also, the defendant threatened to call Al Millard, Walker County Sheriff, and Paul Griffin across Lookout Mountain," the lieutenant said. Mr. Blevins later said he thought it was going to take their intervention to get him out of his predicament.

SHERIFF ALLISON BLEVINS PASSES AWAY

Allison Blevins served as sheriff of Dade County, Ga for 17 years

from 1955-1972. He died in January, 1990 at the age of 84. He was preceded in death by his wife, Maggie Castleberry Blevins. She passed away in the Dade County jail in 1964. The death of the sheriff was an end to a great ride by the family and friends. He left behind many stories and memories that continue to be talked about every day. I hope you enjoy these stories as much as we have.

BLEVINS FAMILY STORIES

This is a collection of stories about our family. Some of the names have been changed to protect the guilty. I know every family has members that do crazy things. We never gave up the chance to have a good laugh at the expense of each other. There are some things that just have to be said the minute something happens because the opportunity may not come again.

JERRY'S FACE

Let me start with the distance from my Mamaw's house to the house I was born and raised in. There was a dark spot between the houses. In that dark spot was a mail box. The idea was for all four of us to leave Mamaw's porch and run to my house. Four of us left and only three made it. We all looked at each other and said, where is Jerry? We ran back and there was Jerry lying on his back at the mail box. His face was the same height as the mail box. He had hit it at full speed and it laid him out. One good thing; the mail box had more damage than Jerry's face. He was revived by placing a cold rag on his face and everything was ok after that.

LINDA'S PROBLEMS

Linda was the middle child. She always insisted she was adopted. I think my mother spanked her so many times she thought no one really loved her. We probably added to that situation by telling her she was adopted.

She was walking up the lane toward the barn and several dogs were following her. Every step she took she stopped and proceeded to call them every kind of SOB she could think of. Uncle Joe again. Mother just happened to be close by and you guessed it, she got her rear end torn up.

I hope I cannot get sued for telling this stuff. I hope not because it is so funny and shows what a great family I was raised in. But I am about to lose my train of thought…

Picky was not the word - when Linda was three or four she had to have her pot warmed. We are talking country now. We did not have an inside toilet until 1955 and I will tell you how we got it later. Back to the warm pot. Betty and Gin hated to warm the darn thing. The fire place was burning down to red coals and the fire was warm. Can you tell what's coming up? Betty and Gin decide to really warm the pot. They stood the pot on the coals and it got red hot. Linda marched in and plopped down and popped up in one motion with the pot hanging on her butt. It burned a ring around her butt. Mother heard all the screaming and thrashing in the living room. She raced into see the results of Betty and Gin's project to break Linda's habit. She saw the ring around Linda's butt and it was not a game.

MOTHER'S PUNISHMENT

I have no idea what mother did to those two, but I am sure it was not enough punishment for what they did. Oh well, it was said it did not break her from having her pot warmed. I am sure she did not use it for a while until her ring healed. We can only be thankful there was no DEFAC then.

The fire place in our house was used for everything besides keeping us warm. My mother always kept a jar full of buttons. Linda had them down playing with them one day. Mother was afraid she would swallow one of them so she pitched them in the fire. Linda in her sweet Uncle Joe way thought mother had left the room and started talking to herself. She said, "that old SOB knew I want those buttons." Needless to say Linda received another one of mother famous whippings.

Ps. All these things were happening before I was big enough to do my meanness.

JOE THE VETERINARIAN

Joe was a self-trained veterinarian. I had gone with him to doctor a farmer's cow. The cow was in the barn and could not get up. Joe had this special mixture laced with moonshine he had picked up at the jail. I don't know what else was in the bottle. He had a quart whiskey bottle full of this "stuff". He opened the cow's mouth and poured the stuff down the cow's throat. The cow laid there in shock for a second or two then jumped to her feet. Joe opened the stall door and the cow headed for the pasture. "I told you I would get her up." Joe bragged. Some fifty feet away from the barn the cow falls over grave yard dead. She had a heart attack and killed over. Joe didn't charge the farmer his usual vet fee. The farmer stated "well at least she is out of the barn."

About 10 family members had gone to a all you can eat place in Rossville. The minute our rear ends hit the chair we ate like hogs. We never looked up. We had been chowing down on fried chicken, barbecue and several vegetables. No one notice Joe turning blue. He was choking on a piece of chicken. He finally got his self unchoked and proceeded to chew all of us out for just sitting their pigging out and letting him choke to death. Joe complained after he got his wind back and proceeded pigging out with the rest of us. A near death experience never stopped us from eating.

THE GANGS OF NEW ENGLAND

In New England we ran in gangs. There were always 15 or 20 of us in the community. We were out at Ewell and Edna's house by the brick church. Snuffy York was with us and had a dip in his mouth. Russell asked Snuffy to give him a dip. It must have made Russell sick. He was lying in a wagon and Linda backed him under a faucet and turned the water on. By the way, Ewell's water supply was sulfur water. Linda turned the water on and washed the snuff down Russell's throat. He was white as a sheet. Linda pulled him to his house and went in and told Pearl her boy was outside in the wagon and he was dead. Pearl ran out and there laid Russell white as a sheet. She got him up and he threw up dry chucks of snuff. He finally got it out of his system and lived another day in New England. I don't believe he asked Snuffy for more snuff again.

SNAKE HANDLERS

Every year this group of religious snake handlers would set up a brush arbor in our county near the Alabama line on Highway 11. One Sunday night after our church let out a group of us went to watch the handlers.

We were all standing in the back of the brush arbor watching and listening. Ginger always had long sharp finger nails. My Uncle Joe was standing about half way up toward the front trying to get a better view of the proceedings. Gin sneaked in behind him and reached down and pinched him right above the heel with her long finger nails.

Needless to say Joe flat footed across the bench in front of him and yelled. Everyone turned to see what was going on. The snake handlers thought Joe got the Holy Spirit. Joe turned a death white. Gin thought he was about ready to pass out. I think we went home right after that happened. Joe said something about changing his clothes.

We were all sitting on the front porch at the jail. Joe always had a saying for everything. The home demonstrating agent came by. She was sort of ugly. Joe said, "Would you look at that? I bet she has to beat her face to make it go to sleep."

JOE'S CURE FOR BEING SCALDED

Joe was so raw between his legs, he could not walk normal! He was talking to a friend who told him to take rubbing alcohol in his hand and slap it between his legs. He said before he could get his hand down he had crap in his hand three times it burned so bad. One does not have to think very long to picture this.

A DARE

The frost on the ground looked like a young snow. The tracks on the railroad looked white there was so much frost.

We were all in grammar school. There were fifteen or twenty kids in New England waiting on the school bus at Browns Store on Highway 11. Being kids, we wandered away from the store waiting for the bus. Actually, we keep moving trying to stay warm. It was just about time for the bus to come when someone bet Dale he would not stick his tongue to the top of the railroad track. Dale never would take a dare. But this time he fell down on his knees and it was like a magnet. You know when your hands are wet and you pick up an ice tray from the fridge? His tongue gripped the track like it was glued.

Someone yelled "here comes the bus!" Our driver, you could be running across the road and he would leave you standing by the road. You had to be in line. Dale moaned, and tried to ask our help. Try talking and hold your tongue. You get the idea. Dale gave one yank with his head leaving the top layer of his tongue laying on the track. Dale talked like he was holding his tongue for about two weeks. To this day no one knows or admits who dared Dale or yelled here comes the bus.

JOE'S VISIT TO INTENSIVE CARE

One of my most embarrassing moments happened at the hospital. Joe was in the intensive care unit. We took turns going into see him every 30 minutes. I had just gotten off work and had not eaten all day. I took the next turn to go into see him. They had all kind of EKG wiring running to Joe's chest. I walked up to the bed and told Joe hi and I didn't feel good. The next thing I remember I was laying across Joe and him yelling for nurses to see about this boy. His devices went wild. They got a wheel chair and wheeled me out to the waiting room white as a sheet. Scared Joe half to death. I was not allowed back in the ICU anymore while Joe was there. They got Joe calmed down and he was told I was okay.

LINDA KILLS THE BIRD

Linda always seemed to do things that would worry her for days.

Linda and Rex Blevins

Take for instance the killing of a bird. We had all made ourselves flips. We had been shooting rocks at the power poles, the side of the mill, and anything that moved. Linda said "see that bird perched on the power line?" Linda cut down at the bird hitting it square in the head. It was deader than four o'clock falling to the ground. Naturally, she fell to the ground screaming "I didn't mean to hit it!" We all cleared out giving her no sympathy at all. She could not do that again if she tried a hundred times.

SHERIFF BLEVINS' 4TH OF JULY BAR-B-Q

The first Fourth I can remember started at my Aunt Nerva Lee's house. I recall whole hams and shoulder was placed on a large pit to be cooked. The meat would be turned over and over and as the heat cooked the outside, it would be sliced off. This process left a great barbecue taste on every slice. It would be continue until the whole ham and shoulder was cooked down to the bone.

This tradition started in the late 40's and continued until the sheriff past away – in January 1990. He did all the planning and inviting of the guests. The family never knew how many people would show up. We never ran out of barbecue, vegetables, desserts, or lemonade. Speaking of lemonade it was made in a 30 gallon crock that was confiscated from a moonshine still. Sometimes there was a hint of moonshine taste in the lemonade, but no one complained.

Dad would invite anyone he knew or saw weeks before the Fourth. All law enforcement personnel were top on his list to invite. This included former sheriffs and other retired persons. Even with all the politicians he had a rule, no political speeches, union talk, or religious discussions.

The barbecue cooking starts on the third of July and continues all night. There was always 50 or 60 people to show up for that. James Hall's family was always there to help. They brought fresh bacon which ended up in BLT's. I can still taste that treat. They used to make a huge peach cobbler for the cooks on the third. This cookout was not for the weak or anyone on a diet.

After the meat was cooked and chopped it was put in a huge black iron pot and simmered until dinner the next day at 12.

I remember there were always at least 200 to 300 people every Fourth. The kids always had a good time as well as the adults. No one that I knew of left hungry. It was always 5 or 6 before the crowd cleared out. The only ones left were family members to clean up, which usually took two days.

One side story that struck me funny involved Lucille word. Lucille, Pearl and I were walking to what we call Pump Park and a bird crapped on Lucille. She turned to me and said, "Rex you know I have been crap on all my life and this just proves it." It did not stop her from eating and enjoying the barbecue.

Dad always used a pitch fork to turn the meat. He said he always washed the pitch fork before using it. No one questioned him about that. He always spent a lot of hours on his feet, but he said he always enjoyed every minute of the day.

Another side story was a group of hang gilders stopped and got out to eat. They went through the line, filled their plates, and asked the sheriff where do we pay. Dad told them there was no cost just sit down and eat and enjoy the music. I recall they were some of the last ones to leave.

The 300 guest enjoyed food they described as "fit for a king," among other things. The annual Blevins barbecue is no more but the memories are still with a lot of people. The music was always presented by Johnny Wallin and his group; bluegrass at its best.

FAMILY TERRORISTS

Back to my three kids. It was graduation day for Craig. The house was full of company from North Carolina. We were all trying to get ready and get to the school. Leigh Ann was in the bathroom and Craig wanted in. Leigh was sitting on the pot with her feet against the door. Craig pushed the door and with one move the commode and Leigh Ann slid back, as the water gushed out and it proceeded to run down through the ceiling on to the floor of the entrance to the house. We left everything and wadded out through the water on our way to graduation. When we came back most of the water had been absorbed up by the towels we spread out before we left. Gee I love those kids.

LEIGH ANN LEARNS TO DRIVE

Back in 1984 Leigh Ann needed a speech for one of her classes. I suggested she do one about her learning to drive. We sat down and just went through her experience we had while she learned the ropes about driving. The title was "Leigh Ann Learns to Drive." There was only one problem; she could not read the speech without laughing. She decided there was no way she could do it.

Since we worked on the speech and it was good I decided to put it in the sentinel. She had no knowledge of my doing that. She found out at school when some of her teachers mentioned seeing it in the paper. I could not leave this out of this book.

> Dad insisted on my learning to drive in a car with a straight shift or stick. 'If you drive a straight shift, you can drive anything,' he said.

> After starting the car, or before you must push in the clutch, or give everyone in the car whip lash. The clutch has been, and still is, my most difficult object.

> Dad said, 'Let it out and mash on the accelerator simultaneous.' We looked at each other and I asked the dumbest question. 'What does simultaneous mean.' Then I got a ten minute lecture on what I have been learning at school.

> After this lecture, we lurched forward as the screaming started. Dad said the radio had to be off so I could hear his yelling. I'm not sure if his yelling or my driving causes his tension headache he insists he gets every time I get behind the wheel.

He has only let me drive on the main road once. The rest of the time I drive on the side road by our house.

I have several problems which consist of remembering to change gears, mash in the clutch, pushing in the brake and slowing down before making a ninety degree turn.

All I was doing was turning into the drive. Dad was yelling mash in the clutch, now the brake, and change into first. During all the confusion I forgot to slow down.

I started to laugh and lost all control. Dad pointed out I was the only one laughing in the car. He insisted I get to the nearest house to let him out.

We also go to the industrial park to drive. I have to stop at all roads, use the turn signals, stop at the railroad and look both ways.

My first stop I learned to lay rubber. Not surprised, Dad pointed out that was not the way to cross the tracks. I started to do my usual, laughing. Stopping on the other side of the tracks, I received another lecture about whip lash, 'New tires are not cheap and the car has over 95,000 miles and can't stand this treatment.'

As we made our way through the industrial park, I continued to receive instructions at a rapid pace.

The big thing now is my 15th birthday and you guessed it, I'm getting my learners permit. I pointed out that I could drive on the highway. I'm not sure what the groans meant when I told Dad. I think he is worried now since there will be two teenagers in the family on the road. I'm learning in spite of the instructors yelling which he insists he has the right to do as a parent."

A WRECK

I started to get worried once I realized there would be two teenagers in the family on the road. Plus, there is 9-year-old Amy who wants to change gears and sort of drive. I am surprised I let any of them drive after the following incident.

I was at a political meeting in Trenton when I got a call from the children's mom with instruction for me to come home and see what my children had done. All of a sudden they were my children only.

When I got home I did not notice the wall in the new room was smashed in at the bottom. I went into the house and three kids were sitting on the couch looking guilty. My first question was "what did y'all do?" They did not say anything. Their mom said, "You did not see the wall in the new room?" I went to check the damage and saw the result of Amy's driving. She and Craig came up the drive way and she did not stop the car. Craig tried to get to the brake, but he was about two feet late.

I told all three to get their butts upstairs and we would discuss it tomorrow. When all were upstairs and their doors closed I heard Amy's door open and heard money hitting the floor. I told her that wasn't enough to cover the damage she had done, and to close her door and get in bed.

The next morning nothing was said. I called Hugh Blevins and he showed up and repaired the damage.

PEOPLE OF NEW ENGLAND, GA

NEW ENGLAND CITY UNDERTAKING IN 1890

In the 1890's an enterprising group of New Englanders decided to develop the coal and iron industry in north Georgia. They chose a site of operation in Dade County, named it "New England" and never got to a conclusion of their financial aspirations.

A bare 14 miles from Chattanooga, it was a tremendous undertaking. They had 10,000 acres of iron lands and a town site of 1,400 acres. Almost nothing remains of the effort today.

From an extremely rare booklet one notes that the officers and directors of the New England company were all New Englanders, with the exception of one Georgian and one Alabamian: Thomas J. Lumpkin of Trenton, Georgia, and George J. Hall of Stevenson, Alabama. The first was an attorney and the second was the superintendent of the Jackson Coal and Coke Co., evidence of Yankee ingenuity if one ever saw it.

New Englanders were glad to have a Georgian to explain that state's rather singular law system, and what could be better than having an experienced miner in the region to begin operations? One of those who sketched and surveyed the site of New England City is W. E Brock, a Spanish-American war veteran, who lives at Trenton, Georgia, where he is a leading citizen.

The opening paragraph of the brochure reads: "this favored locality has all the silent, picturesque beauty of the fair country. Nowhere else is there such a real picture-land framed in so balmy and bracing a climate a happy mid-region between the rigors of the north and the languor of the south. The bounding streams as clear as beryl are never stilled to icy death, but sing their sibilant songs all the year through. Fertile valleys glow, amber and green, in the sunshine. Far dim, majestic blue spurs tower into the heavens; still more distant shadowy purple ridges, misty and somber, seem to rim in the region from the outside world. No one who has ever lived near these grand primeval temples is ever content away from them. There is an exaltation and serenity born of the mountains; every other prospect is in contrast flat and monotonous...."

Then a bit later, follows a description of "New England City," one that never got off the drawing board; "the city site comprises 1,400 acres of land beautifully located in the center of a great mineral quadrilateral formed by Nashville, Knoxville, Atlanta and Birmingham. The site is on rolling land, drained by Squirrel Town Creek, which crosses it at a point most convenient for drainage and for supplying water for manufacturing purposes. A large portion of New England City slopes gradually towards the creek, while the more distant portions rise into rounded hills, which afford lovely locations for residences. About 500 acres have been surveyed and laid out into town lots.

OOM DAYS—Many oldtimers of Dade, area and elsewhere will hasten to say that e New England Community many years ago was "on the boom." A variety of big usiness was carried on and long-range plans were constantly being made for xpansion. These facts have been previously brought out by The Sentinel in giving storical data related to the community. Shown is Ex-Governor Roswell Farnham of ermont, President of New England Company (on white horse directly in front of ation, right). The picture was taken sometime during the year 1889-90. This copy of e old photo was given to Ewell T. Brown of the Brown Lumber Co., New England, y Edward H. Farnham, grandson of the governor, to which mention is made in the oregoing. Others shown on horseback are assumed to be industrial promotors from orthern states. (Photo courtesy of Ewell Brown)

AVENUES AND STREETS

The avenues, which run north and south, are 80 feet in width, while the streets, which run east and west, are 60 feet wide. The blocks are 500 feet long and 300 feet deep. The business lots are 25 feet by 144 feet, while the residence lots are 50 by 144. A narrow alley runs between the lots at their rear. The streets which run east and west descend to Squirrel Town Creek and give fine natural sewerage. The fall from the center of Massachusetts Avenue, at the Hotel State of Dade, now nearly completed, to the surface of the water in Squirrel Town Creek, a distance of 1,200 feet, is 23 feet. The principal avenues and streets have already been graded, and the work is progressing rapidly. Lookout Creek flows to the east of New England City, and is watered by bold and gushing springs which flash out from the hillsides and valleys."

A composite map showing the plat of the proposed New England City, a sectional map and an area map is folded in on the inside back cover of the brochure. The plat is most ambitious, growth being indicated from an area stretching from almost as far north as Wauhatchie to as far south as Rising Fawn. The sectional map shows the Pennington, Castle Rock and Dade coal seams in Sand Mountain and three undetermined but very hopeful seams in the side of Lookout Mountain. Lines indicating iron ore deposits stretch across the entire valley. The area map shows New England city to be in the center of a quadrilateral formed by Nashville, Knoxville, Birmingham and Atlanta.

NEW ENGLAND PLANS WATER AND SEWER

The New England adventurers planned a water works and sewerage system, a dummy line and electric lighting, the same company putting in the latter to provide telephone and telegraph services. The post office and express office were reported as already having been established. Grading of the principal streets and avenues had already been accomplished.

The Stevens house was completed and boasted 25 rooms. The Hotel State of Dade, designed to take care of a hundred guests, was under construction. The W.G. Morrison residence had been completed for some time. This home was west of Lookout Avenue. Space for Taylor Park was reserved near the H. V. Taylor residence and the company promised to donate sites for a school and a church.

Lumber, building stone, brick, lime and sand, plus red, brown and yellow ochre for paint, are announced as being abundant. Building would be a snap.

It would seem that New England city has everything necessary, not only for good health and the foundations of wealth, but she has within her borders all that is required to build houses, from the rock in the foundations to the paint on the outside.

The end of the summary reads, in a sentence, "Anything that helps Chattanooga must aid in building up this city founded by able and strong men from New England."

As one thinks about this vanished financial dream one is reminded of the vanished cultural dream that envisioned Rugby, undertaken some 20 years earlier.

Both enterprises were destined to failure. Maybe it is an indication of the triumph of the spirit that more of Rugby, Tennessee remains.

LIFE IN NEW ENGLAND 1941-1950

First of all let's get the location of my New England. It is not the New England states of Massachusetts, New Hampshire, Maine and Connecticut. My New England is in the heart of Dade County, Georgia.

I have lived in the same area for 73 years except for two years at the University of Georgia, 6 months in Houston, Texas and 3 years in Uncle's Sam's army. I was stationed in Washington at the Pentagon.

Some of the stories told to me starting in 1941 were told to me by relatives and friends. If you can believe it, there have been nine generations of us living in New England on the same farm.

From 1941 to 1946 I cannot remember a lot of what went on in the town. Actually it was and still is just a wide place in the road. There was always a gas station and grocery store, only the location keeps changing.

It was July, 1941 and the rain was coming down by the buckets full. Everyone at the Blevins house was laid up sleeping, or as my papaw would say "y'all going to lay up there 'til the sun shines up your ass and warps your ribs." All my family had such a way with words.

Uncle Joe, who lived across the street yelled at my dad to see if anyone was up. "You going to lay up there and drown." It was raining cats and dogs the day I was born. The water was knee deep in the front yard of our house. It was lapping up on the front porch.

This was the day I decided to come into the world. My life has been one storm after another ever since. Needless to say I was born at home. I weighed in at 9 or 10 pounds. Doctor Gardner was staying at my Mamaw's house across the street since I was due anytime.

I was king bee in the community for almost a year before my cousin was born. I was the apple of my Uncle Joe and Aunt Pearl's eye until then. She could roll up a pillow or blanket and pretend it was a baby and it was said I would raise cane until she put it down.

RUSSELL'S BIRTH

After Russell's birth we all settled into our own homes to start the process of growing up. The farm I was raised on was something else. It was self-sustaining. It was our life and living. It was great to have that background. It was family owned. This means everyone who could hoe, drive a team of horses or plow went to the field to work. This included the women folks. I could not do any of these things then or after I got older. I could never find a hoe to fit my hand. The joke was that everyone who did not enjoy the act of hoeing was not a good hoe-er.

My mother would take me to the field and find a nice shade to lay me under. She would bring a pallet to lay me on while they 'hoded' a round. She would check on me after each round to see if I was still there and alive. My sisters and cousins loved to hoe. They weren't good hoe-ers either. Since I was not active during this time let me tell you about some of my kin folks.

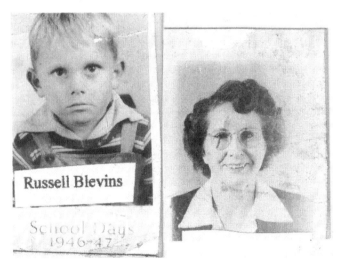

Russell Blevins age 5 and mom Pearl Blevins

My grandmother's house, or I should say my Papaw and Mawmaw, was the center piece of our family. It seems like everyone eventually went through that house. They were great grandparents, cousins, aunts and friends who lived there. It was a hospital, boarding house and good place to get a great meal. Meals were available any time, day or night.

The school was across the street from their house. If the creek "got up" some of the school children stayed because they could not get home. The Brown kid hoped the creek would get up so they could stay at the Blevins'. There seemed to be room for everyone. No one was ever turned away that I heard anyone say. The girl who lived on the hill in back of our house told me she always stopped in Mamaw's house before and after she went to school. She said she always picked up a biscuit and put a streak of lean bacon in the biscuit for a snack. We all did that when we were hungry. Putting mustard on it made it taste even better. My great grandmother was bed ridden for years and partially blind. The girl on the hill was Estell. My great grandmother Paralee made quilt tops to bide her time. Estell would go through and thread needles and stick them in her pillow. She made hundreds of quilt squares.

These quilts squares turned into close to a hundred quilt tops. Before her death my aunt Buelah Mae opened a trunk belonging to my aunt Ersaline that had 25 or 30 of the quilt tops Paralee had made. I took these tops and had a quilt made for each one of my kids, and one for Tonya when she got married. The tops were made between 1927 and 1932. We could not be sure when each was made. They made a great keepsake.

The two-story house still stands across the street from my dad's house where he lived until his death in 1990. Like I said before the house was the center of our family. These are memories that I hope I can remember and put into words.

THE MILL HOUSE

There are several things that are gone now, but they are still in my mind. The area around the house I knew as a kid was 'the block.'

The mill house was where we ground our own meal and flour. Neighbors would bring their corn to have it ground. We rode our bike round the block or just walked around and talked.

The house where our family started still stands and has a lot of great memories. The two story house with the porch across the front and half way down the south side was the place to gather for great conversation and just visiting each other. The porch was the scene of many events. Making kruat, breaking beans and shucking corn where just part of the wonderful times I can remember. I can still hear my Mamaw telling Aunt Mae "why Mae that's a lie." Aunt Mae never lied she just stretched the truth 'til it hurt. Then there was Papaw sitting on the front steps whittling ax and hammer handles. Mostly I remember the shavings on his lap and the apples he used to keep in the cellar rolled up in newspaper to preserve them.

Boy, that cellar was a place so dark and musty smelling. We never went down alone. One always walked down the steps without touching the wall. There were always slugs on the wall. All the summer canning was stored along with apples and other fruit of the season. During the rainy season the cellar would fill up with water. The canned goods were not damaged at all. The water rising up the steps was something we just had to look at. We wondered if it would ever go down.

UP STAIRS IN THE FAMILY HOUSE

The upstairs at the house was a sleeping area for family members, teachers, visitors and anyone else that needed a place to stay. There were teachers who boarded there while they taught at the New England school.

I can still see the platter of stricked meat and cold biscuits on top of the wood cook stove. Everyone that came though that kitchen believed it was bad luck not to get something to eat. Sometimes, to make it extra special, baked sweet taters were there to be peeled down leaving a handle on the end. It was just that kind of place. Everyone wanted to come by. It was warm, friendly and the gathering place for the community.

The fences and gates are all gone. The large trees shading the whole front yard have died, but not the memories of running and playing there.

I remember hearing the family talking about sickness, death, birth and family get-togethers in this one place. I remember the Sunday dinners and the white table cloth spread over the left overs. Boy, the number of times I have stuck my head under the cloth looking for something to tide me over until supper. The food was not reheated at supper, but we did not mind, it was just as good cold.

The long bench is still there. Five or six kids use to sit there to eat. There were two large tables, one in the kitchen and one in the dining room. Sometimes both tables were full and people would have to stand to eat. Meal time was and still is our family favorite time to get together. We have been known to be eating a meal while planning our next.

The fence surrounding the house kept farm animals out and dogs, cats, chickens and other farm pets in. The yard was full of rose bushes, holly hokes, violets of all colors, and flags of yellow, red and white. All are gone now.

THE LANE TO THE BARN

There was a lane by the house that ran all the way from one side of the block to the other. It was used for running farm animals to the barn. I recall my dad telling me that my papaw tried to learn to drive a T model in the lane one time. He ran into wash pots that were always set up beside the lane. He rammed them and told my dad to move the dang things before he hurt somebody. I understand he ran over a sheep in the lot by the house. I believe he gave up driving after this.

The building across the lane from the house was called the shop. The shop had a forge, work bench, and all sorts of hand tools to make the necessary repairs on the farm equipment. One of my jobs was to turn the blower on the forge to heat up metal or horse shoes. We used to turn the handle faster and faster then turn it loose to rest. Usually we tried to grab the handle again before it stopped and jammed our fingers. We had a friend, Cad Vans, who used to come down to the house to shoe our horses. He sort of had a drinking problem, but could he shoe horse? Yes he could. He also had a problem cussing. All of us kids had to stay in the house until he got through. The family was afraid we might pick up some cuss words.

The shop was also used to build coffins for neighbors who died and could not afford one. I can still see the brass handle and pine boards being assembled. It just seemed that anything that happened in the community my family got involved and tried to help. I recall them building a small coffin for a baby that had died. What was really strange the mother had carried the baby around for several days before she could admit her baby had died. My papaw handled this situation with true love and helped

70

her through this situation. These life situations cannot be taught from a book.

The shop had a wood shingle roof that leaked, but it did not really matter, it did not affect the dirt floor. The walls inside and out were covered with plow points, horse shoes, and other items that would be used to repair something. Nothing was ever thrown away. There were wagon rims and other metal junk piled outside the building that rusted away because tractors replaced the wagons. Some of these items are now used for decoration in my cousin's yard.

TWO BARNS ON THE LANE

There were two barns on the lane. The first one next to the house was the milk barn. I remember my Uncle Joe milking the cow and I was peeping through the crack of the stall wall. All of a sudden my face was full of warm milk. He could squirt the milk ten or twelve feet. He used to feed the cats the same way he filled my face. I did not lick it off like the cats did. He was the only one laughing by the way.

Inside the milk barn in one corner stood a large wooden box called the salt box. It was where the salt pork was kept. The process of curing the meat consisted of placing the meat (hams, shoulders and side meat) flat in the box. There was a layer of meat and then a layer of salt. It took several weeks for the salt to take. This process cured the meat and kept it from spoiling. How the meat got to this point will be explained in the next few paragraphs.

Every thanksgiving was the time our family banded together to kill hogs. The vat where the hog was scalded to loosen the hairs was next to the shop. We always killed at least 5 or 6 hogs. There were three or four families that depended on the meat through the winter.

We always complained about having this on thanksgiving. We had to cut the fat or lard. Everyone would get so tired, but we still had a lot of fun. We never made it through the day without someone hitting someone in the face with a flabby sow belly. Everything was so greasy anyway. It would take a week to get the grease washed off.

EARLY START FOR KILLING HOGS

We started early in the morning and would not finish until late in the night. Most of the time we did not actually finish until the next day when we cook the lard.

The tales that were spun around the fire while the lard was cooked in three large black pots! When the cracklins had turned a golden brown, the grease would be squeezed out, and everyone would eat them until it made us sick.

The second day we also ground the sausage. Our lunch consisted of light bread, mustard and sausage. We called them sausage burgers. I was fifteen before I knew there was such a thing as a hamburger. We had a small frying pan with a long handle that was used to fry the burgers in. This same pan was used to dip the cracklins out of the hot lard to put in a strainer. The grease was put into 5 gallon cans. It would cool and turn into lard. This lard was used to cook everything. Chicken, pork chops, corn bread, biscuits and okra and anything else that had to be fried. Good is not the word.

Mamma always cooked lunch or supper at hog killing time. It consisted of tenderloin, hot biscuits, mashed potatoes and, of course, gravy. I can still smell the good scent coming from the old wood cook stove in her kitchen. We always ate a lot of fresh pork when we would kill hogs. After eating a lot we would sit around and watch each other's blood pressure go up. We did not know at the time what made our blood pressure to go up and cause us to be lite headed.

Maggie Blevins scraping a hog.

GINGER BREAD ON HOG KILLING DAY

Mamaw also cooked ginger bread on hog killing day. It was some of the best you ever stuck a tooth in. I have never found anyone that can make it like Mamaw could. It was so dark and moist. We have never been able to figure out how she made it. It could have been the wood stove or the molasses she used. It could have been the home made butter we smothered it with the minute it came out of the oven. By the way we made our own butter.

Allison Blevins gutting a hog.

Back to my barn stories: The other barn was used for farm animals, wagon, plows and a crib where corn was stored in the fall. It was also a place for corn cob fights. We always started with rules in our cob fights. No wet or cobs that had mud on them. This rule did not last very long into the fight. Before the fight was over we were using mud balls, rocks, walnuts, wet cobs and anything else we could throw. This is the tale my dad told me. He also said sometimes they ended in a fist fight.

I had several interesting experiences cob fighting myself. My cousin had built himself a hay fort right in the top of the barn. There was a support rafter right above his head. When he stood up the rafter would almost touch his head. Once he stood up and drew back to throw, but as his hand came across the top of his head the rafter was exactly where his hand and the cob would be. Get the picture, his throw came to a sudden stop when his hand hit that rafter. Needless to say we moved in for the kill with him at the point of death. There was some blood involved, but that happen in the heat of battle in cob fights.

Then there was the time we finished cob fighting and we decided to swing out of the barn. We made it out of the barn the first time, so we tried it one more time. One, two we swing out for the second time. One kid turned a flip and came up holding his arm. The next day he shows up with casts on both arms. He broke both his arms and in the same place. When we got home and our parents heard about what happened you would have thought we broke his arms and left him lying in the hall of the barn to die. This and other dangerous things did not stop us from climbing in the barn and having great cob fights. Do kids still cob fight?

BETTY AND GIN

My sister and cousin, that would be Betty and Gin, were holy terrors growing up. It was said one would think of something to do then both would carry it out. This incident happened in the lane that I wrote about. There were always horses around in lots next to the lane. One of the horses liked to have his rear end scratched. One of the two scratched the horse by the fence. The poor thing really enjoyed it, but unknowing to the horse while one scratched the other tied the horse's tail to the fence. This was bad enough but then they beat the horse with a plank. He nearly yanked his tale off. It is not known at this time what their papaw did to them or else no one will tell me.

Then there were guineas that hung around in the lane. Betty and Gin chased one up and down the lane until it fell over in the barn yard dead. They both claimed they did not kill it because it podaraked one more time when they caught it, then it fell over dead.

Betty and Gin Blevins; notice the socks and shoes.

CLEO BLEVINS, TEACHER IN NEW ENGLAND

Cleo Blevins was a teacher at New England school in the 1930s and 1940s. She was part of our family who lived in Deer Head Cove. She boarded at Mamaw's house. She was very neat and liked everything in its place. She would line up her shoes under her bed in a straight line. Betty and Gin could not leave that situation alone.

They would sneak into her room and proceed to push one shoe out of line. This would cause Cleo to go bunkers. I'm sure she knew who did it, don't you think?

Cleo Blevins Teacher At
New England School 1947

As I said before, our Uncle Joe lived across the street from our house. He always slept upstairs in his birth day suit, that is, naked as a Jay bird. There was no bath room upstairs if he had to relieve himself he would haul it out and let it fly out the window. Betty and her date were sitting out front in the drive way. The moon was shining and it was so quite one could hear a bird fart. All of a sudden the sound of an abundance of rain on the tin roof, except it wasn't rain, it was Uncle Joe relieving him. There was no place for Betty to hide and Joe surely was not hiding. Where else can you hear a story like this except in New England at the Blevins compound? What a family!!!!

NEW ENGLAND METHODIST CHURCH

In the late 1800s, investors from the New England states came to Dade County to mine iron ore and coal from the hills and mountains. A city was laid out with sites for park, school, church manufacturing, business and beautiful residential sections.

Among our earliest recollections is that of the New England Methodist Church. The building of the church was a monument to community cooperation. People of all faiths, as well as those with no specific religious beliefs, worked on the building.

According to stories told by older members of the community, money was hard to come by in those days and contributions of ten dollars or ten days work were made by the men of the community in their time.

Time passed and the project lagged because of lack of money. In order to complete the building, it was deeded to the Holston Methodist conference, now the Chattanooga district, with the understanding that anyone was to be permitted to attend or hold services there.

One article found concerning the church states that it was built in 1897. Courthouse records, Trenton, Georgia, show that ex-governor Roswell Farnham and his wife, Mary, deeded lot no. 1 block 82, on New Hampshire Avenue to Thomas Cummings,

Herschel V. Taylor and W. G. Morrison, trustees of the New England Methodist Episcopal Church, South.

This is recorded in deed book "m" pp. 598, 599 and 600. The deed was executed March 1, 1898, in Orange County, Vermont, and recorded in Trenton, Georgia, April 5, 1898, J. R. Acoff, clerk.

Following this entry in the same book, the New England land company had deeded lots no. 3, 5, and 7 in block 82 to the above mentioned trustees for the church.

To us, this was the most magnificent building in the whole wide world. The walls were of red brick. Light filtered through heavy stained glass windows. The high ceiling was beautifully patterned in wood. Inner doors were padded in green material studded with large brass tacks. The slate roof was topped by a large belfry capped by a tall, slender spire reaching heavenward. It brought high, happy thoughts just to look at it against the sky.

The pulpit raised a few feet above the main floor was encircled by a heavy, highly polished chancel rail with padded kneeling board covered in rich, red velvet. In the center front of the pulpit stood a magnificent hand carved stand covered in red velvet. This was the work of a man from the New England states, probably Boston, Mr. B. B. Chadwick, a member of the Lutheran Church. A memorial window was dedicated to him. Two lamp stands were placed to give light by oil lamps. A claw-footed table stood in front ready for sacraments.

Behind the pulpit stand was a padded bench designed to seat three people. All of this furniture remains in the building today and is very dear to the hearts of many Dade County residents outside the present community as well as those who live here.

Many activities were carried on here from time to time. From 1911 until May 27, 1933, the building was shared by the Methodist and Missionary Baptist on alternate Sundays, with the

Primitive or Hard Shell Baptists sometimes preaching on the fifth Sunday. In all cases, the congregation was the same, regardless of denomination.

New England Community Church Sunday School Class 1898

Point of interest: I started first grade in 1948 at this church. Elizabeth Owen, my cousin, was my teacher. This was a story in itself. I was supposed to have started in 1947, but I refused to go, if you can believe a 7 year can do that. I paid dearly for it. My mother took me to school, which was just around the corner from our house, one block. I would beat her back to the house and be sitting on the porch. This went on for several weeks then Uncle Joe came to my rescue. He said "Maggie he is not going to school." So she told him I could come to his house every day and stay until school was out. Two weeks before school was out Joe and I were in Chattanooga and I saw two cops. I asked Joe why they were looking at me. He said because they were wondering why I was not in school. I told him if he would not let them get me I would go to school. So, the next morning I got up and went to school. The bad thing about that, school only had two more weeks before school was out for the summer. Mother wanted to beat my butt because of this. Two weeks to go and I went to school. The next year I finally started without any problem and graduated in 1960.

Back to the New England Methodist Church.

FIRE DESTROYS MAGNIFICENT CHURCH HOUSE

New England, May 12, 1936: The bare brick walls are all that remain of the beautiful church house at New England, as a result of a fire which broke out during an electrical storm.

Lightning, it was thought, struck the steeple of the building and within a short time the raging flames, fanned by a strong wind, were far beyond control. Practically everything, including piano, stove, benches and stand were saved by those who had rushed to the scene. Also, the windows, which were very rare in design, were saved, excepting one.

The fire was first noticed by J. L. Blevins, who stated that immediately after the bolt of lightning had hit, a blaze was seen in the upper part of the belfry.

The magnificent building was erected in 1897 and only a very few of those who helped in the building are now alive. Material used in the construction was of the best, and many say that its duplication would be almost impossible.

The corner stone, behind which is said to be a list of the names of those who assisted in the construction of the building, and several pieces of money, was unmolested by the fire.

PEOPLE OF NEW ENGLAND

There were many interesting people who lived in New England. One was Aunt Theny Brogden.

Headline: Old Resident Dies as Age of 103. "Aunt Theny" Brogden, (Colored), Age 103, Died At Her Home At New England On August 1934.

She had been a resident of Dade County for the past 85 years, and was a typical old "mammy negro." Surviving were two sons, Frank, of Tiftonia, Tennessee, and Floyd, of New England; two daughters, Mattie Cole of Wauhatchie, Tennessee, and Laney Brogden of Pittsburg, Pennsylvania. Interment will be in the Sarah's Chapel Cemetery. Floyd her son was also buried in Sarah's Chapel Cemetery.

She was very much a part of our family from 1910 until her death. She was always at my Mamaw's house each time Mamaw had a baby. Floyd worked with my family on the farm.

When she first moved to New England she was a slave. My family never mentioned that in any conversation I can remember them having. Her house was on our property that my great grandmother purchased in 1910. They lived there until her death.

Cards of thanks were printed in the local paper and read as follows August 2, 1934:

> We wish to thank our white friends, and colored, for their kindness shown us during the illness and after the death of our loving mother. Also Rev. W. M. Larr, for the lovely funeral sermon preached. We thank our white friends for the beautiful floral offerings; also for the sweet music rendered. Words cannot express our thanks. We pray God's blessings upon each and every one. Your kindness will never be forgotten.
>
> The family: Mattie Cole, Floyd Brogden, Frank Brogden, Fannie Brogden, Claude Cole.

A very interesting side story to the Brogden's family: There were several listings of Brogden in the Chattanooga telephone book. I decided to call the first one listed and to my surprise when I told him I was from Dade County, he was delighted. After a few minutes talking to him I felt like we knew each for years. I mentioned Aunt Theny's name and he said "man we have been looking for you for years." This was the contact his family needed to trace his family roots.

After several months of arrangement, the Brogden family met in New England for a tour of the old home place where Aunt Theny lived. We toured the cemetery where their families were buried. I also gave them a brick from the fire place where she cooked their meals. The pile of bricks was the only thing left of the place.

There were twelve family members that came down for the meeting. They asked questions about how we knew her and her sons. It was great that we were able to connect them with their family roots. We had marriage license, birth certificates and death records to give the group.

LANDMARK COLE HOME IN SLYGO VALLEY DATES BACK TO 1850

One of the more interesting landmarks in Dade County (and there are few of them around these days) is the Cole home in Slygo Valley.

One of John Cole's sons, William Isom Cole moved to Slygo Valley in 1850. The original house, built of logs, consisted of two large rooms and a huge fireplace of cut limestone, the spring house was also built of limestone. This spring was to be the water supply for New England city in the late 1800's. The home has remained in the Cole family since 1850. Jane Allison's, grandparents, Robert Allison, born in 1849 and 1852, respectively, both received their

Cole plantation in Slygo, 1850s

education at the Cole Academy, as did some of their older children- the late John Allison. Jane Allison Blevins born in 1874, my Mamaw, also received her education there. She later taught school there at the Cole academy. Here is a copy of her teacher's license:

TEACHER'S LICENSE.

Jane Allison Blevins teacher's license, July 6th, 1897.

The original copy hangs in the Dade County Board of Education building. It is dated July 6th 1897. It is the oldest Dade County teacher's license that can be found.

COLE SPRINGS

Cole Springs--Slygo Late 1800's

Cole Springs located in Slygo. It was to be the water supply for New England city. Part of the spring house continues to stand. It was located by the Cole farm.

"The big white oak" later cut in New England in 1904. It lists a who's who that lived in the New England area. Pictured is Bill Brown, Joe Brown, Floyd Brogdon (Theny's son), John Mayhew, Bob Wilson, Frank Brown, Dave T. Brown, Tim Raines, Lee Forester, Em Blevins, Joe Jobe, Ben Derryberry, Carrol Derryberry, Chris Avery, Tom Dickerson, J.L. (Jim) Blevins, H.V. Taylor, John Raines.

A group of young people that were in Gus Forester Sunday School Class at New England Baptist.

J C Holmes, Christina Porter, Larry Forester, Shirley Debter, Betty Blevins, Shirley Keel, Charles Bryant, Martha Bryant, Virginia Blevins, Roy Gearrin, Cloia Mae Gearrin, Louise Bates, Bettye Derryberry, Genine Stove, Lindia Blevins, Aubrey Forester, and Gus Forester

Ladies who made up the sowing circle that met in New England once a month. It included quilt making and always a covered dish lunch.

Mennie Forester, Pearl Blevins, Mrs. Gene Bates, Ruth Tatum, Dewitt Williams, Maggie Blevins, Mae Combs, Dora Forester, Cecil Raulston, Martha Derryberry, Girl UNK, Bobby Raluston, ,Joe Lee Tatum

Allison Blevins family in 1945.

The Lockmillers Tourist Court located on Highway 11 in New England in the 1940s.

Dr. T.J Lumpkin who lived in New England City. He was kin to Chief Justice Clark of the Georgia Supreme Court. I furnished Chief Justice Clark other pictures of his family of which he showed them from the Bench of the Georgia Supreme Court.

The New England City School, students who attended that school in 1911 and the old pump where they got their drinking water. This pump was also part of many water fights through my childhood.

Top row: Grady Wilson, Byron Lawson, Bunyan Austin, Glenn Simpson. Second row: Raymond Doyle, Crit Lawson, Allie Wilson, Ruth Forester Tatum, Edna Forester Reeves, Allie Snodgrass, Eula Holmes Cole. Third row: (Unknown), Earl Holmes, Tom Dagnan, Sula Holmes Mitchell, Delia Brown Peck, Sarah Forester Holmes, Cliffie Hixson, Ida Hancock Wallen, Bessie Derryberry Walston. Fourth row: Cleave Austin (Principal), (Unknown) Phillips, (Unknown) Phillips, Buelah Ruth Jones, Ersaline Blevins Carroll, Etoka Blevins Beckhem, Pearl Holmes Wheeler, Laura York, Gertie Lee Smith Wallen, Inez Hughes, Lydia Brown Mayes. Fifth row: (Unknown) Phillips, Allison Blevins, (Unknown) Lawson, Roy Brown, Henry York, Middleton Cuzzort, Sam York, Charles Hixson, Price Jeffrey, Joe Blevins, Dock Hancock, Thomas Grady Hughes.

Sentinel Staff Photo

OOPS!—It doesn't require professional photography to see that this is a double exposure. Nevertheless, both photos are unusual. The object, of course, is an old-time hand pump. It is located in a well where the old New England schoolhouse once stood back in the days of yore. It still pumps water. The dimly-seen berries are "white blackberries." They grew at the back of the Allison Blevins home at New England—were ripe at the time the picture was made—tastes the same as ordinary blackberries, but are white, not black.

BLEVINS ANCESTRY: 1800-1991

BLEVINS

Richard	1800-1870
Jonathan	1817-1911
Emerson	1854-1929
Jimmy Lee	1874-1947
Em Allison	1905-1990
Rex Allison	1941-
Craig Em	1968-
Cody Allison	1991-

RICHARD BLEVINS

Jonathan Blevins, son of Richard and Rhonda Scott Blevins, was born in Kentucky on July 17, 1817. He married Emily Maxwell in 1837. Jonathan and Emily had thirteen children.

Emerson Blevins was the 10th child of Jonathan Blevins. Emerson was born in 1854 in Dade County in Johnson's Crook, Georgia on August 31, 1854. He worked as a blacksmith. He married Paralee Smith from Deer Head Cove in DeKalb County, Alabama. She was born on November 7, 1853. Emerson died April 28, 1929 and is buried in Payne Cemetery, Trenton, Georgia. Paralee died March 16, 1937 and is also buried in Payne Cemetery.

Point of interest: Paralee fell and broke her hip in the late 1920's. She laid in bed for several years at her home in New England, Georgia. She made quilt tops to pass the time away. Several of the quilts tops have been made into quilts and given to her great, great and great, great, great grandchildren. Some of these grandchildren continue to live here and are our eighth generation of Dade County, Georgia residents. Amy Blevins Cole, Chase Cole and Cassidy Cole each received one of the quilts and reside on the farm where Paralee lived and died in New England, Georgia. Leigh Ann Mcbryar, Haleigh and Aleigh also received one of the quilts and reside in a nearby house on the same farm.

JIMMY LEE BLEVINS

Jimmy Lee was born February 4, 1874 in Keller, Texas. He was the son of Emerson Blevins and Paralee Smith. He married Laura Jane Allison on March 8, 1903 in Trenton, Georgia. He was a blacksmith and farmer.

Laura Jane Allison born June 29, 1874 was the daughter of Robert Benson Allison and Minerva Elizabeth Derryberry. Jimmy died April 17, 1947, and is buried in Payne cemetery, Trenton, Georgia. Laura Jane died Dec. 8, 1958, and is buried in Payne cemetery, Trenton, Georgia. Jimmy Lee and Laura Jane had eight children.

The children were: Ersaline, Allison, Etoka, Joe, Nerva Lee and Beulah Mae. Reba was born on February 17, 1910, and died July 27, 1910. Lonnie Rey was born April 22, 1918, and died September 6, 1918. These two children are buried in Payne Cemetery in Trenton, Georgia.

Papaw and Mamaw (Jim and Jane), Beulah Forester, Ersline, Etoka, Allison, Joe, Nerva Lee, Beulah Mae

Beulah Blevins Forester, Jimmy Lee Blevins, Jane Allison Blevins

On the steps of home at New England

Jim and Jane Young Children: Allison, Joe, Etokia, Beulah Mae, Ersline

Jim Blevins on Longhorn Steer in Grapevine, TX

Em Blevins, member of Trenton
Academy basketball team, 1920s.

Allison, son of Jimmy and Laura Jane Blevins, was born at New
England, Georgia on September 27, 1905. He died on January
15th, 1990.

Allison Blevins and twins Lennie and Lemmie Castleberry, his best friends.

He is buried in Payne cemetery in Trenton, Georgia. He married Maggie Castleberry, daughter of Benjamin and Malinda Bridges Castleberry. She was born October 15, 1911 in Rising Fawn, Georgia.

She died on December 27, 1964, and is buried in Payne cemetery in Trenton, Georgia. Allison and Maggie had three children: Betty, Linda and Rex.

Four Generations: Paralee, Jim, Allison, and baby Betty Blevins

BLEVINS ANCESTRY

This is a historical genealogical record of the descendants of
Richard   its that
are a par

This is a copy of our coat of arms. The Blevins Coat of Arm is
officially recorded in the ancient Heraldic Archives.

This building was located on the site of Shaw plant.
My family lived on this property until 1910,
when they left to move to New England City.
"OLD IRONWORKS" Late 1800's

The Blevins family came from Fromby, just south of Southport on the west coast of England and Wales. It is believed that the patriarch of our Blevins line was a William Blevins who came to America in the late 1600s and temporarily settled in what is now the state of Maryland.

It is believed the entire Blevins family left Maryland in the mid 1740's for the southwestern section of Virginia. William Blevins, born 1735, died in Sullivan Count, Tennessee in 1825.

RICHARD BLEVINS

Richard Blevins was born in 1800 and died in 1870. The line of descent for Richard Blevins is not known for certain, but from the previous data given in "A Glimpse of Early Day Blevins", one feels almost certain he is a descendant of William Blevins born in 1735.

Our information about Blevins' descendant comes from a census record and Denver Blevins of Sand Mountain, Alabama. Richard

Blevins and Rhonda Scott were both buried in Deer Head Cove Cemetery in Dekalb County, Alabama. Their son Jonathan Blevins was born July 17, 1817, and married Emily Maxwell. This is the start of the Blevins family that I have written about. Jonathan died October 22, 1911, and is buried in White's Chapel Cemetery, Grapevine, Texas.

EMERSON BLEVINS

Blacksmith shop in Keller, TX, early 1880's – John Hartman, Emerson Blevins (Jonahthan Blevins son), and E. Rogers

Emerson Blevins had the first blacksmith shop in Keller, Texas, but after some years decided to go back to Dade County, Georgia. He lived here the rest of his life.

Emerson Blevins 1854-1929

Arrival in Texas

After arriving in Texas everything seemed to be going fine until
Emily Blevins, wife of Jonathan Blevins died on May 1, 1878.
Jonathan Blevins later married Mrs. M. L. Curre at Grapevine,
Texas. She died April 9, 1882. He then married Mrs. M. E.
Trentham February 27, 1884. But this marriage was unsuccessful
and ended in divorce in 1886.

JONATHAN BLEVINS 1817-1911

Jonathan Blevins was the son of a circuit riding primitive Baptist preacher born on the American frontier in Kentucky on July 17, 1817. His father, Richard Blevins, believed the work of God should go forward with the advancing frontier.

Jonathan Blevins 1817-1911 and Emily Maxwell 1820-1878

The family stayed only a short time in Kentucky. They moved to Alabama in Jackson County. Census records show they were living in Marion County, Tennessee. They lived there until 1839, then moved to Deer Head Cove community of DeKalb County, Alabama.

Jonathan Blevins was married August 27, 1837 in Marion County, Tennessee to Emily Maxwell. Records shows that in the mid 1850's the family moved into the Dade County area. Jonathan's son Emerson Blevins was born August 31, 1853. Records do not show if he was born in Dade County or Jackson County, Alabama.

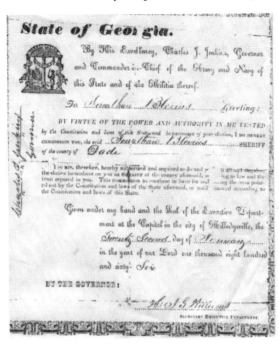

Jonathan Blevins was elected sheriff of Dade County: served from 1856-1872

Emerson is our second record that continues our family history. He was a part of the move to Texas in the 1870's.

Jonathan Blevins was a small man. He was approximately 5 feet and 4 inches in height, and weighed at the most 140 pounds. It was said a size 6 shoe would have been large enough for his foot. In his later years he was described as carrying a walking stick, but seldom using it. Yet this small guy was man enough to be the sixth sheriff of Dade County, Georgia. He served in this capacity for 16 years, being elected for eight – two year terms. (1866-1873). In the late summer of 1873 he resigned this position to find a "greener pasture".

As sheriff the duties he had to perform were often times distasteful and required tremendous amounts of physical and mental stamina, and the courage to carry out the law he had so faithfully sworn to do. Two incidents of the many he was faced with are of interest.

Incident no. 1: Once he was required to pick up a man on a warrant issued for the man's arrest. He took along with him an extra horse for the man to ride back on. After traveling for some distance to the man's place he found him and his wife in the field hoeing corn. He approached them; stating his purpose for being there and explained to the man by law he was required to take him in. The man hurled with the hoe handle striking him across the nose and knocking him to the ground in a stunned condition. He soon gained full control of himself and took the man in without further provocation. Upon examination, the nose was found to be broken. He later remarked the man could have easily beaten him to death from the daze he was in.

Incident no. 2: Dade County, Georgia was a slave holding community of the south, and often times the hardships the slaves faced here were no different from the problems they had in other parts of the southern states. In his first years as sheriff, a very gruesome incident occurred. A Negro slave had taken her two small children to a spring and drowned them. The slave's master reported this to the sheriff, and he went out to the plantation and picked her up. She was placed in the jail and kept for trial. At her trial she admitted to drowning the children, and explained that she could not face seeing her children grow up in the cruel world of slavery. This woman was sentenced to be hanged by the neck until dead, and as sheriff his duties also included being hangman. A coffin was prepared for the woman and placed in the back of a wagon. The woman was driven to the spring where she killed her children to face her death. On the way she sat on the top of the coffin singing, "Lawd, I want more religion". When they arrived at the spring he placed a rope in a white oak tree and fixed the noose. As she was standing on the coffin with the noose around her neck she shouted, "Lawd, I'ze know a nigger is got a soul." The wagon was then pulled forward.

After the hanging the master came to the sheriff wanting him to do something with his slaves. He said they were refusing to work, and felt if he would only go out and talk to them; he could probably scare them into going back to work. He went to the farmer's plantation, but to the surprise of the farmer, he talked sympathetic to the slaves.

He explained to them this was the law for all mankind, and if he did what this lady had done, he too would be hanged. He told them of the lady admitting before a jury what she had done, and this was the framework in which the law worked, and as sheriff it was his duty to carry out the law regardless of how unpleasant it was. He talked for some time with the slaves, informing them he was not a slave holder, and did not believe in slavery. But, as the law allowed slavery, they would have to make the best of it.

Rex Blevins at the tombstone of Jonathan Blevins,
his great, great Papaw, buried in Grapevine, TX.

Dade County Sheriff 1838-2016

Deputies listed under sheriffs without dates.

1838-1846 Unknown

1842-1846 Leroy Sutton

1846-1852 Zachariah O'Neal

1852-1855 Joseph Killian

Deputy Hugh McKaig

1856-1862 Ansel Smith

1863-1865 Frances Daniel

1866-1873 Jonathan Blevins

Deputy Shade Stephens

1873 J. W. O'Neal

1873-1874 L. B. Burnett

1874-1878 Jacob Steele

1879-1881 J. W. Blevins

1881-1882 B. P. Major

1883-1884 W. A. Byrd

1885-1886 J. R. Brock

1887-1892 W. A. Byrd

1893-1896 Robert Carter

1897-1901 J. M. Hall

1902-1905 Robert W. Thurman

1906-1910 Robert A. Carter

1911-1918 W. N. Tatum

1919-1921 W. H. Cross

1922-1925 L. N. Holmes

1926-1927 L. S. Newman

1928-1948 Gorver Tatum

1949-1951 Bill Lynch

1952-1955 Cull Graham

1955-1972 Em Allison Blevins

Deputy Bill Breedlove

1973-1976 Charles Morgan

1977-1984 Ronald Steele

1985-2004 Phillip Street

2005-2012 Patrick Cannon

2013-Present Ray Cross

Dade County Civil War

In the later years of the Civil War Dade County, Georgia was plagued with Yankee troops. They would steal everything they could get their hands on and get away with. Jonathan Blevins had several hives of bees, and they kept robing his bees for their honey. So, to "out fox" those Yanks he took a hive of bees and placed them under his bed, drilling a hole through the wall of his log house for the bees to enter and leave the hive. The bee hive was placed as near the wall as possible, and the space between the wall and hive was daubed with mud to keep the bees from being loose in the house.

Also, under Union Rule during the Civil War they were not permitted to have weapons. He had a nice 44 inch hexagon barrel cap and ball rifle, and he was determined they would not get it. So, he hid it in a hollow tree. Later he found that rats had gnawed the stock off. The gun is in the possession of a Blevins family member in Duncanville, Texas.

Three of his sons, Richard, William and Lewis, fought for the Confederacy during the war. They told their mother they were going to church, and slipped off to join the army. The three fought through the war together, and under the command of General Stonewall Jackson until his death. Richard had three horses shot from under him, Lewis was wounded in the leg and Will was hit in the forehead from a ricocheting bullet which went around his head and lodged in the back of his head. He was later captured and taken prisoner. He was kept in a field hospital near Whiteside, Tennessee.

The war claimed the life of Jonathan Blevins' youngest brother, Gaines Blevins. He was home towards the end of the war, and early one morning two Yankee soldiers came to his father's house looking for him. Emerson was at his father's house when they came. They asked for him and went into the house to tell him they were there, and Gaines came out. They told him unless he ran for it they were taking him in. There was a cane patch near the house and they advised him to run into the cane patch and get lost from them. He started and just as he got to the edge of the field they fired the fatal shot which hit him in the back.

In the year of 1871 Stephen Blevins Austin became discontent with his lot in life, and decided to move westward to Texas and take a chance to improve their lives. He had heard about the farmlands of Texas, still untouched by ax or plow. Stephen wrote back to Dade County, Georgia telling the people what a wonderful and beautiful place Texas was. He wrote Robert P. Blevins, son of Jonathan Blevins. Robert married Stephen's niece. Upon receiving the letters, he talked to his brothers and some decided they too would move to Texas. As plans were being made other brothers and sisters joined them. Jonathan resigned as sheriff of Dade County in the early fall of 1873 and the westward movement began. The Austin and Burkhalter families traveled with the Blevins. One man in this wagon train drove a yoke of oxen pulling a two wheel cart. It is said that he arose at sunrise and left camp, and pulled in after sunset to camp during the night with the other families.

This story has no ending. It continues everyday. I had to end it for now so I can get it published. I have not been in a hurry because this story has been going on for 75 years. But I cannot keep waiting for more things to happen before I publish this book or it will never get published!

Thank you to all of you who were involved in this story. This book is dedicated to you. Without you, there would be no story. And even if there were, what would be the point of publishing it were you not there to be honored? Some of you have already passed on to the next life and will not have the opportunity to read this account. Perhaps you are the lucky ones, you who will not know how the story may have been butchered.

For those of you who would beg to differ with this account, you may contact me in the year of our Lord 2050 AD with you complaints.

I am also publishing this book for the sake of my family whom I love dearly. We love to have a good time no matter what life brings us.

The end… at least for now.

APPENDIX: PHOTOS

Maggie Castleberry: Future wife of Allison Blevins, Student at Rising Fawn School

Maggie, Allison Blevins, and Patsy Woodfin in front of the Dade County Jail.

4-H Steer Showing Early 1950s: Russell Blevins, Rex Blevins, Jerry Price
Note: Rex got $90 for his steer which he used
to buy the families first black and white TV.

Victor Quinton

New England Boy Scout Troop #36

112

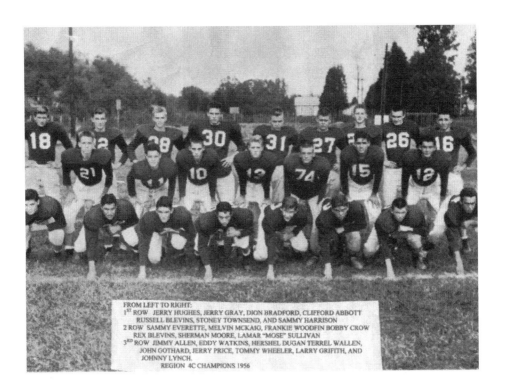

FROM LEFT TO RIGHT:
1ST ROW JERRY HUGHES, JERRY GRAY, DION BRADFORD, CLIFFORD ABBOTT
RUSSELL BLEVINS, STONEY TOWNSEND, AND SAMMY HARRISON
2 ROW SAMMY EVERETTE, MELVIN MCKAIG, FRANKIE WOODFIN BOBBY CROW
REX BLEVINS, SHERMAN MOORE, LAMAR "MOSE" SULLIVAN
3RD ROW JIMMY ALLEN, EDDY WATKINS, HERSHEL DUGAN TERREL WALLEN,
JOHN GOTHARD, JERRY PRICE, TOMMY WHEELER, LARRY GRIFITH, AND
JOHNNY LYNCH.
REGION 4C CHAMPIONS 1956

View of store front showing WWII army recruiting station on the square.

Case Grocery Early 1900's

COKE OVENS OF THE GEORGIA IRON AND COAL COMPANY, COLE CITY, DADE COUNTY, GEORGIA.

Trenton Academy Late 1800's-1927

Cumberland Presbyterian Church

Known to have furnished shelter and sleeping quarters
[f]or a number of Sherman's men, when he "marched through
[G]eorgia," is the Cumberland Presbyterian Church building
[pi]ctured above. This is one of the oldest buildings in the
[co]unty, being built in 1859. Names of many of those who
[ca]mped in the building, during the War Between the States,
[w]ere found written on the inside Walls when the building
[w]as repaired some years ago. Stucco has been put on the
[or]iginal frame structure. The building is located near the
[co]unty jail.
—Photo by C. L. Holmes

Case house down by railroad in 1925

Colonel Nesbit Home 1835

ABOUT THE AUTHOR

Born and raised in New England, GA, Rex Allison Blevins loves Dade
County. Brought into this world by Allison and Maggie Blevins in their
house in New England by Dr. Gardner on July 8th, 1941, Rex has spent
his whole life in Dade county (to date) with the exception of 3 years in
the U.S. Army and 2 years at the University of Georgia. He retired from
Hudson Wire Company, and served as a probation officer for 28 years.
Rex got involved in politics in 1982 and spent 19 years serving the
people of Dade county on the school board and the county commission.

Made in the USA
Columbia, SC
04 January 2025

51024364R00072